Bows, Swamps, Whitetails

Bows, Swamps, Whitetails

Tim L. Lewis

iUniverse, Inc.

New York Lincoln Shanghai

Bows, Swamps, Whitetails

iUniverse books may be ordered through booksellers or by contacting:

iUniverse
2021 Pine Lake Road, Suite 100
Lincoln, NE 68512
www.iuniverse.com
1-800-Authors (1-800-288-4677)

ISBN-13: 978-0-595-41362-1 (pbk)
ISBN-13: 978-0-595-85711-1 (ebk)
ISBN-10: 0-595-41362-5 (pbk)
ISBN-10: 0-595-85711-6 (ebk)

Printed in the United States of America

To someone who cherishes our swamp woods and its denizens and all the days we've passed among them, Breanna Rachelle Lewis; my dearest hunting pal.

Faint as a stream's voice murmuring under snow,
Sad as a love forever more deferred,
Song of the arrow from the Master's bow,
Sung in Floridian vales long, long ago.

Will H. Thompson

Contents

Introduction

Something was moving. The undulating creek surface left that in no doubt, but the ferns blocked even a glimpse of it. These ferns, richly verdant and thigh high, grow in lush profusion along the many sloughs of the swamp bottom. From my perch in a slender cabbage palm, I waited intently as the ripples danced about, unsure whether to ready my bow or camera. So far during my vigil eight otters had worked past, some with eyes, ears, and nostrils above water, bee-lining quickly down the creek and others coiling, diving, meandering with their supple, serpentine movements, searching for food. An indigo snake had quietly slipped along beneath me, poking into hollow logs and flowing its six foot length under and through the palmettos.

These ripples and rings however seemed to progress too slowly for an otter and were too large for a snake. Time passed. As my curiosity arose so did guesses and thoughts of what it could be. I had several times seen gators and snapping turtles in the creeks, but seldom did they disturb the water so obviously. These ripples were substantial, but their source barely moved. Hooded merganzers, wood ducks, raccoons all were possibilities. Raccoons searched along the streams at a faster pace than this usually, but sometimes wood ducks bobbed and splashed about an area for an extended period of time.

Then, on the far side of the narrow creek, beneath the wall of ferns and vines, came a movement of muted brown and grey. Perhaps it was a wood duck hen. My binoculars revealed a head with antlers just above the water's surface! Immersed in the creek, a buck was walking its edge and stretching its neck to pull off the fern and greenbrier leaves. He browsed steadily, but moved so little it seemed he would never approach even though the little creek ran within two yards of my stand. Fern fronds interfered with a good photograph, but my binoculars allowed me to study his palmated eight point rack of ivory and grey. He was content to move little, surrounded with bountiful forage and hidden almost entirely.

After what seemed to me like hours he abruptly waded to my side of the creek and scrambled up the bank. He remained motionless in the ferns 25 yards away for a good minute and then shook vigorously, haloing himself in a cloud of spray, and proceeded to walk to the wild orange tree ten yards north of my stand.

Although none of its sweet oranges were lying under it, he nosed about and several fallen leaves disappeared as if by magic into his mouth like dust balls into a vacuum cleaner.

Over half an hour had elapsed since I first saw his ripples and the whole time the wind had been steady and favorable and now, with the buck so close, I wanted to wait for an angling away shot. His greyish body quartered toward me at seven yards when the feather tied to the tip of my bow stretched slowly toward him. The wind had switched and in a bare instant there would be no shot at all. I drew and 'Deer Bane's' quiet thump whisked the arrow forward and through the great buck's chest. He was staggered, but managed to lunge across two deep creeks and knowing the wound to be quickly lethal, I silently urged him on toward the swamp's edge for each yard he leapt would be one less I would have to drag and carry him through the water and muck and over the multitude of fallen trees. I was not lucky in that regard for he looped tightly back and fell quite close to my stand.

He was a beauty though and I felt fortunate to ambush him late in the season. The tote out may have been a struggle, but in truth, my memory about it is dim. What I remember so vividly is the surprise of seeing a buck hidden in the water, feeding so secretly and also the ivory look of the wide palmate antlers.

Other memories and experiences flood over me as I think of bowhunting southern swamps. I should tell you of cool days with clear, blue skies over the trees and the rich tones of deep brown and green below. Long, skinny cabbage palms and giant, gnarled oaks, gum trees and cypress with their surrounding bevy of peculiar knees. The rich, full scent of wet, fallen leaves and black earth; a sweet, open aroma which, when breathed deeply, saturates and fills the soul with the lushness and quietness of the swamp. And of windless mornings with thick mists stacked up above the still waters and layers of beautiful white fog blanketing the treeless pastures and later turning golden as sunrays find them. Of spiderwebs sagging and glistening jewel-like with dew. Of frigid, windy days when the gusts carry thick, nearly solid clumps of steam from the sloughes like ghosts, whisking them in tortuous eddies between the tree trunks and through the swamp, suddenly making clear how stories of white spirits came to be. Of bobcats and whitetail deer that slip away as silently and ethereally as the mists themselves. Of hot mornings in the swamp when the dampness causes the slanted rays of sunlight to become visible and tangible as they pierce through any opening or crevice in the canopy like translucent fingers of bronze. Sometimes such a shaft will shine on a darkened old stump or fallen log and an odd thing will happen. The damp wood warms rapidly and issues gentle puffs of steam mimicking small bits of smoke from the smoldering remnants of a fire so perfectly that at times I've been compelled to go inspect it to put my mind at ease. The backlit green lushness, the filtered golden rays, and the light breaths of steam on such days make the swamp seem beautifully alive.

I should tell you too of the tweeters of birds and the silent, flitting forms of damselflies that have wings of blackest black tipped with white and slender twigs of bodies that gleam iridescent greens and blues whenever they pass through the scattered patches of sunlight.

I should tell you the swamp is not silent for it is alive with sounds, but the spirit of the swamp is a quiet one.

Read with me now and my hope is that the following accounts will tell of all this and even more about the swamplands I hunt and love.

1

Swamps and Whitetails

The morning had passed quickly as the swamp entertained me, its appearance changing with the angle of the sun. Hogs and squirrels had been constantly present since first light and a pileated woodpecker had shattered great chips of wood from a dead and mist-dampened tree. Big ferns carpeted the swamp bottom with a thick coat of spring-like green and thick gardens of smaller ones softened the rough branches of old oaks. In more vertical trees bromeliads grew and bloomed and orchids hung like unmowed grass.

By 9:15 the hogs had moved on and a low, steady, deep sound began accentuated with continual pops like maybe a distant plane droning and suffering a repetitive backfire. It grew louder and sounded more like a four-wheeler with a backfiring problem than an airplane and probably only two hundred yards away. While trying to comprehend a vehicle in a wooded swamp where none should be, I abruptly realized the noise was emanating from the creek twenty yards from my stand. It was a low, deep throb with burbling pops. Each drone would last perhaps forty seconds. Actually, the source of one drone was the creek directly in front of me and another supplemented it, nearly in concert, from probably seventy yards upstream. All at once, the two alligators quit burbling and roared mightily and repeatedly to one another. Squirrels shrieked and chattered, birds flew and anhingas clucked, but the 'gators heeded them not and bellowed with all their might. The roars were primal and powerfully loud, "Aaaaaaaaugh!" The whole of each monstrous, reverberating bellow was deep, but the ending even deeper. The swamp shook as these two titans answered roar for roar for nearly five minutes. They ended with some prolonged low burbling rumbles and then all was inordinately quiet.

The woods stayed quiet a long time and while nothing moved I sat and watched and mused over how different my last two bucks were, particularly their faces.

One buck I spied in a very overgrown pasture seventy yards off. He had the rusty coat of summer and a long, tall body and neck. I was in the shade of a small, green cypress head to hide from the midday sun. The wind was good for rattling because, with the deep water behind me, it was likely he would angle close before getting downwind. Of course, that is, if he responded at all.

He did respond and walked directly toward me stopping several times to thoroughly thrash small shrubs and once to rub a cypress sapling. I tickled the antlers lightly two more times fearing he was getting so distracted in using his own antlers he may have forgotten these others. Each time he immediately resumed his approach. He was head on until six yards from my tree. His rack was high and colored like varnished maple. It was a taller than average set of antlers, even though it was not really large, but he was large and swaggered in dominantly. His head was extremely long with a grizzled grey muzzle. At six yards, he turned broadside abruptly and his head disappeared into a fringe of myrtles. In mere seconds he would vanish entirely behind them and be screened until he was downwind. Bane Too's limbs bent deeply and sprang forward and the arrow whisked to its mark, striking with a sharp and lethal 'shhrick'!

The trail was easily followed and only sixty yards. He was a big, beautiful eight point buck. His left antler was palmated. His right had a widened knob on the brow point an inch below its tip.

Two days later, I climbed a pine near where a dense cypress head, an overgrown marsh, and a myrtle rich pasture converged. The wind that slipped lullingly through the pine needles was from the north and the sky was a clear, pretty blue. The trunks of the cypress were so thickly covered with lichens that they glowed white in the slanting early light. Cicadas hummed intermittently and other insects chirped and buzzed. Butterflies fluttered and glided past. It was the kind of morning typically associated with increased levels of game activity, yet hours stretched on and no game showed. I may have felt antsy if I was not so busy updating my journal.

The myrtles were thick and numerous enough that they disallowed much of a view except for windows here and there. At ten o'clock, a deer moved through a little such opening three or four hundred yards away. My glimpse was fleeting and the head was hidden, but the body seemed large and the direction was upwind.

I rattled loudly and viciously and after a couple minutes rattled again and waited as patiently as one can when the chance for a buck might be forthcoming. Fifteen minutes elapsed and my hopes diminished. Perhaps I should have remembered how the buck from my prior hunt had stopped every couple yards to hook some brush or rub a tree as he came in to the antlers, but instead I thought about that it may not have even been a buck and it was awfully distant.

I sat down to resume writing. Before any words could spill onto the paper, he was there, eighteen or less yards off and walking deliberately toward me! His antlers were wide and tall and square. Moving in slow motion, I stood, traded journal for bow, and balanced my stance. He walked quickly and passed broadside at eleven yards, but by the time I was ready he was quartering away at eighteen yards maintaining his fast pace. I drew Bane Too without consciously aiming or leading and the speeding blur of the arrow found its mark.

He was a beautiful and symmetrical eight-point with much longer tines and wider and longer main beams than the first buck. He fell in a natural pose with his head up. After propping the head with a slender branch to exaggerate slightly its erect position, I clicked a couple photographs. If I hadn't laid my bow on his back, a viewer would think the pictures were of a live bedded buck. His face was short, with a nearly black muzzle and light swaths of creamy brown around his eyes and nose. His neck was thick and heavy and the throat patch was also creamy. The outside portion of each ear sported a bright white patch.

The first buck, although his antlers weren't as impressive, was taller and outweighed the second by twenty-two pounds. When the front edges of the ears were lined up evenly, the first buck's nose extended fully three inches further than the second's and, laying the extracted jaws side by side, the distance from the back of the third molar to the front of the first premolar was greater by an inch for the first buck. However, the second buck was five and a half years old and the first only four and a half. (By the way, on both the private and public lands I hunt, the deer jaws are gauged for age by wildlife biologists.)

For a long time, I had considered the length of the face as an indication of age, but these two bucks demonstrated dramatically that this may not be the case and muzzle length may be related to genetics or perhaps how early in the season a buck was born or how much nutrition was available during his first summer. Regardless, both of these bucks were beautiful and each was fairly dominant in its area.

A year before, I bided an afternoon from the same pine. It was a hot October and the all time heat record was exceeded at least four different days. A short downpour quenched the late afternoon heat and the breeze freshened from the east, deliciously cool and pine scented. A small 'gator repeatedly captured and devoured frogs in the shallow marsh about the stand and I caught glimpses of three does between the thick stands of myrtles.

After a bit, a bobcat strode past. No sound or movement heralded his arrival. He was suddenly there, a nonchalant apparition, silent, but extremely aware. He was gone before I could video him so I squealed against the back of my hand hopeful the sound might tease him back. A few minute's wait gave no indication of success so I bleated like a distressed animal.

Five does pounded up at full speed, stopped momentarily, and raced on beyond me. Another bleat lured them to the base of my tree where they stood, perfectly radiating the essence of whitetails; the alertness and inquisitiveness of these creatures, their beauty and grace, all somehow conveyed by their poised, but ready posture, their swiveling ears, searching eyes, and long delicate white whiskers around the eager, inquisitive nostrils. In their watchful state, they nosed about for a long while, but eventually began feeding. I have no idea what became of the bobcat, but my bleats yielded plenty of excitement and beguiling images branded into my memories.

A December afternoon caught me in a maple in the Bull Creek swamp bottom. Beneath the low cabbage palms and between verdant tracts of ferns, it looked like the very floor of the swamp was in motion for a great congregation of ibises pulsed about, their combined grunts creating a persistent din. The mass moved amoeba-like, flowing between trees and through the creek channels. The individuals birds groped along and the huge flock milled in varied and ever-changing directions. The giant group was composed of many smaller flocks and the individuals gave no evidence of loyalty to any one band following any bird close at hand.

Most of the unit flocks had one or more egrets included in it. The egrets are sharper-eyed and warier than the ibises and thereby offer the ibises an elevated degree of safety and I assume the gropers, moving like a flood, spook food to the egrets and so benefit them. With the continual pig-like grunts of the ibises and the egrets' harsh croaks they were a noisy lot and, as interesting as they were to observe, I felt more like I was hunting when they were finally just a murmur in the distance. Afternoon began to give way to evening.

A barred owl hooted and I mimicked it. Another owl called and I responded again. The female landed silently in the tree above me and the male fluttered over her back and bred her, hooting hysterically all the while. This was the third time my owl calls provoked a romantic episode above me and I caught this occasion on video.

Four gobblers pecked by to the southwest. Hopeful, I stood and readied myself and my bow. They never approached my stand area and as they disappeared, I rehung Deer Bane. At my movement, a deer blew behind me and I turned to see a nice buck bounding away.

His blows had barely dissipated when a doe fed from the north unconcernedly, browsing until she neared my stand when she began sniffing for acorns. She was quite close a couple times, but because of her angle or intervening brush no opportunities for a shot came until she was walking away at an angle at twenty yards. Drawing until the back of the broadhead contacted my left index finger, I released the sibilant shaft. It disappeared into her with a quiet 'thunk'. The hit was behind the rib cage, but with her quartering angle, I felt it should be okay. She ran fifteen yards, stopped, turned around and hunched up. The hunch, a manifestation of a gut shot, worried me. My binoculars failed to reveal any gushing blood or even blood on her side. She was about thirty yards from my stand and swamp trees blocked clear arrow flight. After a ten minute wait, moving with utmost stealth for her head and eyes appeared quite alert, I stepped onto the seat of my stand. From that vantage, if the aim was perfect, an arrow might reach her. I hesitated, my thoughts jumbled and opposed. A second arrow could secure her and save her anguish if my first shot had hit only guts. At the same time, a miss would ricochet loudly off the sheltering trunks and without a blood trail, a spooked deer would probably be a lost deer. I bent Deer Bane and aimed, but my confidence wasn't there for such a long shot with so demanding a tolerance. I eased the tension from the string and stepped back down to the stand's platform.

A minute or two later she decided things by walking to the northeast. The trees obscured all but a sketchy image of her movement, but there was about a two foot gap directly in line with my first shot. When she stepped into the alley she was forty yards away, but there was little time to think as she was moving and there would be no other openings. The arcing trajectory of the arrow which sprang from Deer Bane's able limbs looked good and the 'thunk' once again spoke of a pass through, but it was impossible to tell in the diminishing light. She raced north and fell within forty lengths. With daylight nearly gone, no flash-light, and a deer to tote, I assembled my gear and climbed down immediately.

The doe lay with her left side up and it had a single hole one-third of the way forward from the back of the ribs. I could find no other holes and concluded that my second arrow missed and struck a rotten log or something to create the 'thunk' and the hemorrhage from the first wound, aggravated as she ran, finally accounted for her collapse. After fifteen or more minutes of fruitless effort, I resolved to search for my arrows another day as darkness had enveloped the swamp. Even at mid-day, the adjoining treetops shade the understory and render the swamp dim and when the sun sets, the faint light vanishes abruptly.

Anyone who has been under the lush swamp canopy in the blackness of night can testify to the magical charm of the great multitude of sparkling fireflies, their green and white flashes flickering about and glowing from all directions, even high and low, tantalizing glimpses that seem like a galaxy of tiny, cool stars near at hand. Through this enchanting beauty, I dragged the doe, untroubled by the logs, cypress knees, and other obstacles that trammeled my progress, happy to be burdened with a deer that, despite her mortal wound, could easily have proved troublesome to find.

When I dressed the doe, the wound on her left side displayed an x-like shape. I used two bladed broadheads that day so, suspicious, I flipped her about and dis-covered two wounds on her right side, one behind the ribs and one through the ribs. The first arrow had caught her liver, diaphragm, and one lung. The second, which entered through the first's exit wound, double lunged her. In retrospect, I probably would have had a blood trail had I retrieved a flashlight and searched for it, but if not for the second arrow it likely would have been a long and arduous one.

In early archery season, late one afternoon I climbed into a stand in some scrub and saw two deer a few hundred yards away near the swamp edge. They fed and cavorted and then one ran off and the other watched. I finished adjusting my gear and readying Deer Bane and sat down to wait. The distant deer were gone.

Because of the thick nature of the scrub, there were only a few small openings where deer would be visible or through which an arrow could fly, but to its favor, the scrub acorns generally ripen before any others and therefore the game congregates there. As soon as I sat little sounds came from behind me and I stood back up slowly and carefully. A doe and yearling stepped through the only open lane behind my stand at ten or twelve yards, but I wasn't ready in time and didn't see them again until they were forty yards to the northeast and continuing further. I bleated and the reaction was instantaneous. The doe raced westward and stood facing a cypress head about thirty-five yards off. My bow was in my hands, but I yearned for a camera because all aspects of the scene were perfect. The late afternoon sun illuminated her obliquely defining her chest and head, and the white of her throat, face, and ears shone brightly against the rich, verdant background. The posture of her neck, head, and ears characterized the alertness for which deer are venerated and, to top it off, sunlight sparkled in her eyes and shimmered from a viscous, clear strand of saliva dangling twelve inches or so from her lip and swaying in the breeze.

I bleated again and she ran to me and stopped once more twelve yards from my stand and under one of the largest oaks. Deer Bane murmured, the arrow whispered its quick answer and the doe was stricken.

While waiting for deer, a hunter gets to witness many out of the ordinary things. One December day as it grew light in Bull Creek squirrels began to move. This wasn't surprising as thousands and thousands of water oak acorns were dropping that year and squirrels were all through the swamp. This day, however, the squirrels seemed loosely associated in groups of four to seven individuals chasing one another around in single file, across logs, around the trunks of trees, up trees, down trees, into and out of holes, and among roots with very little of the shrill chattering that accompanies the faster chases of two or three squirrels. This was a slower, tail waving progression that went from one tree to another and often back. I witnessed no feeding nor nest material gathering. There were seven squirrels in the group directly near me and there were other groups as far as I could see so that the swamp bottom was alive with waving tails and grey motion. All told, there must have been over a hundred squirrels in view from my stand which is a phenomenally high number. I had heard of squirrel migrations before, but these squirrels didn't seem to be going anywhere as much as milling around. There was no mating that I could see and very little contact between individuals. I sat in the same stand two or three weeks later and saw only one squirrel.

Once two otters swam up and caused a great blue heron to fly as they splashed about it. They appeared to do it purposefully and I've seen them chase wood ducks and mergansers as well. One can't help but wonder if it is playful devilry, curiosity, or an attempt to feed. Herons seem unlikely otter prey with their size, incisive eyesight, and quick and dangerous beaks. The otters, however, betrayed no hesitance or hint of caution.

Gopher tortoises are common enough in our pastures and scrubs, but only once have I seen one in the rich and fertile swamp woods. It is a happy tale and worth including.

One Friday I scouted an area in Bull Creek that showed promise. Acorns were falling and plenty of deer and hog tracks were present. Most years it holds many buck rubs, but my gentle style of scouting, trying to stay in the flowing waterways and leave as little scent behind as possible, revealed only a few, none of which were extraordinarily impressive by size of the sapling, but some of which had been worked vigorously. Slipping from the area, I passed a scrape at the edge of the swamp that showed no recent activity.

The following week, carrying a spear and Bane Too, I eased toward the stand site. The old scrape had not been tended, but a fresh one was opened near it with tine marks in the sand that showed no sign of dew. Two new rubs were blazed on young cypresses. A big boar was harassing some sows. Their repeated squeals and protestations alerted me to the hogs' presence. The boar had a massive, thick head and was heavily shouldered and probably would push the 200 pound mark on a scale. Anyone who has tried to move a good sized hog realizes how much more difficult it is than a deer of equal weight would be. All of the mass is in one area rather than spread out over the longer legs and frame of the deer. Even though he was a tempting target, an outstanding hog, and a substantial amount of meat, my inclination to launch an arrow was tempered by the travail of the drag and the knowledge that slaying it would abort my deer hunt and possibly foul the site for future deer hunting. Deciding against venturing a shot, I miraculously slipped past and climbed the tree without spooking the hogs.

They fed off and the wind died and the woods became very, very quiet. Nothing, save mosquitoes, seemed to be stirring. The strong smell of cypress nuts hung on the air. After a long while came the sound of something moving. Puzzled, for the sounds were unlike those of a squirrel or armadillo, but progressed so slowly that it was hard to conceive their cause to be a hog or deer, I searched. Eventually, a gopher tortoise pushed his way over mud and fallen leaves and through clutters of sticks and limbs. He was wet, apparently having crossed one or more of the creeks. His progress was slow enough that he was dry when I last saw him and he ate not at all during that time. One couldn't help but be curious what he was doing so far from the usual haunts of his kind.

When he had passed the stillness returned, but after a short bit, the breeze returned and with it the indistinct susurration of the leaves in the trees, the crisper murmur of dying leaves as they tumbled earthward, the quiet 'ffft' of acorns plummeting to the soft, black soil, the hard knock when they hit branches or logs, and the loud swat of them against palm fronds. Owls began to hoot.

A buck stepped out of the thick fifteen yards from my stand and fed within ten yards. Palm fronds screened him most of the time, but I passed on the few opportunities he offered because he really didn't seem any larger than my last couple of eight points and I was down to my last buck tag. He fed diagonally and was obscured by a cabbage palm until he was twenty-five or so yards away. Several hogs, sniffing and crunching acorns, approached from the west. He eyed them uneasily and fed more hurriedly to the southeast. As he disappeared, it struck me he may have been a ten point although I hadn't thought to count tines when he was closer.

The hogs were all around me, some directly below and had I been inclined to use my spear, they couldn't have offered a better target. As they milled around, I tried to find the buck, but he remained gone and four minutes passed. I rattled lightly a few times and waited, sorry I had let an opportunity pass, knowing how seldom a good buck could be intercepted at close range now that rifle season had started. A minute or more went by with nothing but hogs in view. I rattled again, longer this time, gently at first, but a bit more vigorously at the end. One of the hogs, either picking up my scent or becoming nervous of the louder rattling, issued the long growl of warning and a few trotted off a couple yards. The rest looked around.

The buck rushed in at a pace between a fast walk and an outright trot and halted eight yards from my tree. He was alert and may have stopped to look for the 'buck fight', or because of the hogs around him, or possibly he had a faint whiff of me as he was nearly downwind. I drew Bane Too. There is the split instant while the arrow is in flight when the archer knows whether or not his aim was true. Sometimes on longer shots a flight that looks good will sadly drop short, but this buck was close and in the millisecond between the release and strike, while Bane Too was still quietly thumping and the going arrow a streaking blur, I knew the shot was on. I heard the 'chuck' of the arrow's deadly blow, the buck lunged and the hogs scattered.

There was no need to blood trail for the buck fell within sight. He was a beauty; his head regal and large, his pelage with still a hint of summer rust, and his antlers, symmetrical and colored like worn red and yellow leather, adorned with ten craggy tines. He was six and a half years old and turned out to be one of my best bucks ever. The hunt was as exciting and perfect as anyone could ask.

2

Water Up

Florida is quite flat so when we have a lot of rain either from a prolonged storm or from several rains over a relatively short period of time, the water level rises dramatically and erases huge amounts of exposed land. Tropical storms, with their torrential rains, are most common in the fall and regularly flood our hunting lands, sometimes diminishing the dry land by ninety percent. The pastures look like vast sheets of water and when driving on the roads, currents swirl away the muddy wakes behind one's truck and care must be taken to avoid deep spots or eroded gullies. The dirt roads are elevated above the level of the pastures and swamps and are subject to deep fissuring as the water flows across them. Some of these abrupt erosions are no more than jarring nuisances, but some can swallow the front half of a truck.

In one period of high water, my dad and I were startled to spot a large fish swimming on the road. It was similar to a mudfish with the lobed tail and prehistoric appearance, but had more of a bony exterior. This was one day after the storm and the most intriguing aspect was that prior to the rains the closest water was at least half a mile distant.

Fire ants are common here, voracious and tenacious creatures that are small and reddish and pack a surprising sting for their size. They seldom hesitate long in using their sting when their nest is disturbed. High water floods their colonies and when wading across a pasture a hunter can encounter shiny, rust colored balls of them. Apparently the surface tension of the water is sufficient to bear the weight of an ant with its legs spread and the other ants and eggs mound up on top of the ones on the water. I've attempted to get good photographs of these ant balls several times, but they always turned out blurry or out of focus and finally I realized the problem was the incredibly rapid speed with which each individual ant was moving. The colony was motionless, but the surface was in constant blurring motion. Some colonies approached the size of a volleyball and if touched with a stick would instantly envelope it. It would be hazardous to bump such a ball and care needs to be taken when wading to a stand in the predawn morning. By the way, this ability to avoid breaking the water's surface tension also allows these ants to make bridges of themselves over fairly long spans of water, even water that is flowing steadily and this seems quite an engineering feat in itself.

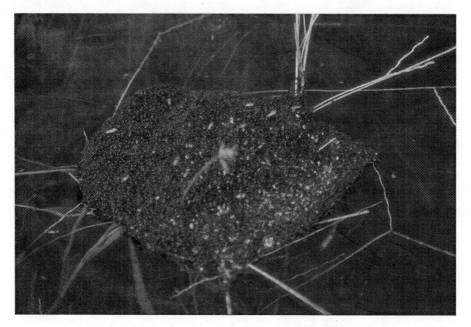

A floating colony of ants rendered blurry by the constant and rapid movement of each ant. Note the eggs.

Whitetails are affected by the high water as well. Not only does it allow them less bedding sites, but it floods a lot of the vegetation on which they feed. Some plants die after being submerged for an extended time and in the swamp bottoms the currents are strong and relentless enough to sweep the forest floor clean of plants so even after the floods recede the shortage is not immediately relieved. However, new growth is not long in sprouting in the fertile black soil of the swampwoods and the deer favor its lushness.

Once, when the water was up, slipping quietly through thigh to waist deep water in the swamp, trying to reach the other side more than still-hunting, I spied a peculiarly shaped cypress and as I endeavored to resolve its shape, a spike slid from the tree and half bounded and half swam away. The cypress trunk split just above the water level and the spike had settled himself into the divide to bed.

Many times, I've witnessed deer in chest to back deep water feeding unconcernedly and once watched a nine-point chase a doe through water as deep during the rut. Loud splashes preceded their arrival near my stand and kept me abreast of their progress for much of the morning as they seemed to favor the general vicinity. The introduction of this book described a buck feeding in water deeper than his back was high. What struck me as most remarkable about this behavior was how invisible it rendered him. The creek side vegetation was so high and the waterway so narrow that from the ground no hunter would have been able to espy him from either side of the creek. Thus secluded, he was able to feed leisurely and if danger presented, and the buck was composed and canny enough, he could have slipped his head into the overhanging greenery and completely vanished. That some bucks are so artful as to choose to hide in water rather than flee, I have no doubt and can offer an example.

Once, heading to our hunting lands and driving past a ranch with cleared, low pastures, I spotted a regal looking buck thirty yards from the dirt road. Continuing on for fear of spooking him, I braked a short distance down the road and turned back, camera ready this time and hopeful of a capturing an image of a good whitetail on film. He was gone. This seemed incomprehensible as the nearest tree line was more than four hundred yards away and at least a glimpse of his bounding form should have been visible. The pasture was flat and the grass short and the only feature at all at variance with the monotony of the newly seeded pasture was a small pond actually closer to the road than where the buck had been standing. The pond's vegetation was a sparse smattering of grasses or thin reeds shin high on a man. My eyes were off the buck for such a short duration that I grasped for any explanation for his disappearance and even though logic would not have predicted the buck to head nearer the road, I utilized my binoculars to scan the pond and he was there, lying in the shallow waters with his head down, but eyes, ears, nose, and antlers up. His eyes were on me and the picture was appealing through the binocs, but, unfortunately, with only a 200 mm lens, my camera didn't provide sufficient magnification and the buck appeared only as a browner area in the vertical, green pond grass. Of note was that during the rifle season, rather than run across coverless pasture, the buck elected to move closer to the danger and rely on being unobserved.

Another example of a buck's tendency to sit tight, although not in water, should be shared. To reach a stand at a thin gap between two cypress heads, I passed a small island of gallberries only two or three yards across, walking along its eastern edge. The wind was from the east. The western edge of the patch bordered the brown, marshy grass that filled the narrow section between the nearly touching domes of cypress. It was in January and deer season was coming to a close. From my elevated position in a cypress, fifty yards south and west of the gallberries, I could see my truck parked distantly in the pasture and watched as some quail hunters parked next to it and let their dogs out. Not eager to sit in the midst of a quail hunt, I climbed back down and returned to my truck again passing the very edge of the low gallberrries. The bird hunters explained they just were going to work one bit of cover to the north that often held a covey and were then moving on, so instead of relocating like I had decided, I trekked back to the cypress walking along the gallberries a third time.

Almost immediately upon my reentry to the stand, two does, spooked by the quail dogs, came from the north, skulking the cypress fringe and its marshy juncture with higher ground, brushing against the little clump's west side. The afternoon then trickled by uneventfully. As the sun neared the horizon, it seemed some movement had occurred in the gallberries, but it was only an impression and my binoculars and four minutes of study revealed nothing. I was convinced I was mistaken, but then minutes later something popped up again. For the next ten or fifteen minutes the pattern was repeated, a narrow, whitish apparition floating amidst the gallberry stems for a scant second. Over time, it lingered slightly longer and one time it appeared wide and different and I concluded it was a calf's face. Yet, why was a calf acting so strangely and why was it so far from any other cows?

Eventually, the phantom stayed up long enough to let me catch sight of it through my binoculars and proved to be a giant buck that had not only already dropped his antlers, but had begun growing new ones, the nubs being large in circumference, but barely more than an inch in length. His face, including the nubs and even the back of his head and ears was a very light creamy color, hardly darker than the insides of his ears, but it was grizzled and grey on his muzzle. His nose was long and he looked old. For a half an hour he would raise his head tentatively and scan the area or stretch his nose up to sift the air, disappearing into the greenery in the interim. This action is what first offered the glimpses of white from the underside of his chin. At length, he rose and moved to the edge of the gallberries gradually over another five minute period, taking the barest and most tentative of steps and then studying the surrounding area, sifting with his nostrils, perking his ears to listen and sometimes lowering himself down again so only his vertical nose remained to be seen. Finally, out of the tiny patch, he lifted his tail, defecated, and then slid through the marsh grass and melted into the cypress north of me. His body was massive. This evening perfectly illustrated the phenomenally cautious nature of a mature whitetail and its reluctance, during the rifle season, to resort to flight despite repeated approaches of a hunter to within a yard or yard and a half.

Along the same line, Archibald Rutledge, in one of his writings, related a time a buck sprang from its hidden bed and as it hurled away, he bowled it over with his Parker shotgun. Other members of his group arrived and they dressed the buck. Later, curious to investigate the cover in which the buck had been ensconced, he strolled to the spot, if my memory serves correctly, forty or fifty yards distant (Rutledge liked to let a buck get the first few jumps out of its system and settle into a run before pulling the trigger) and was dumb-stricken to have a second and larger buck leap away from nearly under his feet.

Hurricane Frances changed the face of our hunting land with uprooted and broken trees, high water, and the remaining trees stripped of their leaves and many of their branches. Someone looking at the trees remarked it resembled winter up north. Hurricane Jeanne followed within a couple weeks arriving in the evening of the opening day of archery season and coercing me from the woods midway through the day in order to prepare our home. The eyes of both hurricanes passed quite close to our camp and the changes they wreaked were tremendous and will alter our woods for many years to come. The initial storm raised the water level dramatically and thereby rendered both the sandy soil of the pastures and the black muck of the swamp softer and more easily displaced so when Jeanne's sustained winds of over one hundred miles per hour and gusts substantially higher pushed and shook and tore at the thick crowns of oaks, the soil let go and the massive root systems were torn from the ground. The curved roots now stand like huge, rounded tombstones over the fallen giants. Many, many trees centuries old were wrenched from the earth and died in this manner and they did not die alone, either crushing other trees with their bulk as they tumbled or yanking lesser trees out by the roots that overlay or intertwined their own. Perhaps 35–40 % of the trees fell and passing through or along the creek bottoms can no longer be described as walking as more time is spent climbing over and around and through the fallen limbs and trees.

Oak trees of all varieties that were not uprooted fared well. They, of course, lost limbs and leaves, but few if any broke in the trunk. Pine trees with their ability to flex survived well overall although maybe five per cent of them snapped. Very few pines uprooted and the breaks that occurred were typically halfway up the height of the trunk. Cabbage palms bend and give (as anyone that has hunted from a stand in one on a breezy day can attest) and almost all withstood the winds untroubled. A small percentage suffered snapped trunks, primarily in the upper half, but by far most that were lost were crushed or uprooted by neighboring trees that fell. I discovered no palm uprooted alone, only those whose roots were entangled with the giant web of roots of huge, toppled trees. The cypresses bore the hurricane winds with apparent ease. I found none uprooted and the only broken ones were again victims of neighboring oaks or maples that fell.

The nearly complete stripping of leaves is interesting for a number of reasons. Initially, it gave the woods a barren, alien, and forsaken appearance, but this bleakness was followed quite shortly by the wildest profusion of verdant exuberance. Leaves, in tender and spring-like shades of green, erupted everywhere. Many trees had lost so many of their branches that leaves sprouted thickly from their trunks and coated them with dense green fur.

Persimmons, cabbage palm berries, and most of the acorns were likewise stripped from their trees. Oddly, the oranges, as big and heavy as they are, tenaciously clung to their trees. This loss of mast must have affected wildlife as it is a huge if not the major part of the fall diet for deer, hogs, turkeys, raccoons, squirrels, jays, and crows. The extreme diminution of numbers of acorns by the wind stripping them from the trees was compounded by the loss of so many branches and again by the downing of so many trees. Therefore, whenever I encountered a tree that still harbored some immature ones, I looked forward to their ripening, confidant that the tree would draw an abundance of game in this year of dearth, but with a few exceptions this was not the case. The great burst of leaves so important to the tree's very survival must have required the lion's share of the stored energy and future generations were less of a priority in this time of stress. The little acorns never matured and when they did fall they were ignored by game, apparently of too little nutritive value.

Following the two back to back hurricanes and one preceding one that grazed us, the water, of course, was exceedingly high and flowing strongly, drowning and sweeping away many of the plants so when the water did recede, the swamp bottom was raw, naked earth around fallen and standing trees. Everything was brown and grey and drab. Like the case with the drab and bleak trees though, this was quite transient and a beautiful lushness reclaimed the swamp.

After the waters receded, when walking about on dry land far from the creeks and ponds, I was once overwhelmed with a stench of putridness and death not unlike that of the ruptured remains of a recently bloated carcass, but no carcass was in sight although I then remembered flushing a buzzard as I headed into the place which was a low spot littered with fallen leaves. After searching more for the dead animal, I discovered the carpet of leaves was in actuality the curled forms of a multitude of small fish and minnows trapped as the water fell and dying helplessly as it disappeared all together. Thirty yards off was another depression reeking as oppressively.

Most of the toppled trees died, but still a good many retained enough roots in the soil to survive. Both the fallen dead and the fallen alive contributed to the nutrition of wildlife. The squirrels consumed the bark from many of the dead ones, busy day after day, but the amount they gnawed away with their tiny teeth was staggering as many of the trees were entirely stripped in three to six weeks and the trees were two or more feet in diameter and obviously quite long to reach through the canopy of the swamp in life. The squirrels preferred the sides of the fallen tree best, the underside second, and the top least although all aspects of the tree displayed their attention and all aspects were denuded eventually. Possibly the moisture content of the bark affected their preference, but it does seem likely that predator avoidance may be a better explanation as the sides afforded them a view above and below and allowed over or under as avenues of escape from hawks and owls or bobcats and coyotes.

The branches of the living horizontal trees were suddenly in easy reach of deer. They responded enthusiastically for these trees too brought forth fresh shoots and leaves. There were so many of these prone trees that no one served as a steady draw to aid a hunter intercept a deer. I did discover three different orange trees that suffered a fall without entirely being uprooted, but it seems unlikely they will survive because deer ate every leaf from them. Had I run across any of them sooner they may well have provided a reliable attractant.

Stalking in the swamp became difficult for a bowhunter. Literally, millions of branches, twigs, small limbs, and leaves were strewn across the ground. Movement was noisy and awkward. With the water's recession, broad bands of this debris (which had floated) formed layers, oftentimes over a foot deep that defied silent approach. To this may be added the hardships posed by the fallen trees, the great tangles of grapevines and greenbrier that tumbled down with them and the soft and muddy holes left beside the upturned roots.

When the waters began to diminish, but were still high, I hunted from a thin and rocking cypress at the eastern edge of a long strand that extended primarily north and south. At 4:30 in the afternoon, a buck crossed the rough and scraggly pasture from the east heading for the cypress. He dallied at a couple spots, but mostly moved purposefully forward. I considered launching an arrow at forty yards, but if he turned north at the edge, I should have a nearly point blank opportunity. On the other hand, if he headed south there would be no path for arrow flight; in fact he would be instantly lost from view. I elected to wait.

He gave the appearance of bearing slightly north, but at the last second turned south and vanished. The slenderness and shakiness of my tree made it risky to attempt to hang Bane Too with an arrow on its string, but it was paramount to have it near at hand and ready so I balanced it on the stand's seat and rattled. No response followed. The wind was from the northeast. Bucks almost always angle downwind as they approach my rattles, but the head was exceptionally deep with water and thick with fallen limbs requiring anything passing to climb or leap through or over them. Bucks are no strangers to thick and tangled places, but this was quite excessive and should be a barrier to an unworried whitetail. If he had circled downwind, noise would certainly have accompanied him even as stealthy as bucks are. I rebalanced my bow as the tree wobbled and swayed in the gusty winds and rattled again, longer and more loudly this time.

With the bow barely back in my hands came the clashing sound of something pushing quickly through dense palmettos and the plashes of deer steps. Then he was only seven or eight yards distant, yet scarcely visible through the heavy vegetation of the head. Surprisingly, after the hurried way he blustered in, the buck paused to nibble a vine and one antler snaked around a sapling and showed five points. A ten point! Hunters know the excitement and the nervousness; a buck that close, but lingering in heavy cover, his current course angling northwest with a northeast wind threatening to carry my scent to him if it varied a few degrees and bearing it to him without varying if he progressed four yards. Directly in his path, happily, was an opening with nothing to impede arrow flight. He ambulated forward and into the opening, but now choosing not to dally. With game so close and the shot seemingly easy, I reminded myself to draw fully and feel the broadhead touch my finger as the hard string tightened against my fingers and Bane Too's limbs began to bend. Despite my own reminders, my aim was imperfect, perhaps rushed because of the certainty of him getting a noseful of me at any second and the arrow pierced him slightly further back than ideal. However, the wound had to have caught at least one lung and drove through him completely. With him quartering toward me, the exit wound had to be in the belly. He scudded to the northeast clearing the cypress and into the somewhat open pasture and then curved to the east and then south, racing with unbelievable speed, tail down and getting it. Just past a lone pine he arced toward the west and disappeared into the acres of tall gallberries. It was possible I glimpsed a bound to the south or maybe he tumbled there.

With a complete pass through and so much of his course recorded in my mind and with the lone pine tree as a landmark, it was likely he could easily be retrieved, but as an ace in the hole, I could call Mack to bring his beagle Skylar if necessary. Mindful that Mack would have to come from Cape Canaveral, close to a two hour drive and with darkness coming in three hours, it seemed prudent to check the blood trail and see how easily decipherable it would prove to be. Incomprehensibly, there was no blood trail. I scoured over where it should be, the beginning where fresh splashes of mud and water betrayed his passage, the curves of his course, the straight portion where he had sped south, and the area of the lone pine. Close to an hour had passed and I decided to extend the search into the tall gallberries where I had last glimpsed him reasoning that if he had tumbled there, he was dead so there was need to fear spooking him and if he had continued fleeing, the cover was thick enough to hide my investigation. My hopes were high despite the unanticipated lack of blood and I crisscrossed determinedly through the area over and over, but it proved fruitless and frustrating.

Hot, sweaty, despondent, I sloshed to my truck and called Mack and was unable to reach him, but left a message. Returning to the stand, I climbed and studied the territory and the landmarks, picturing his departure as vividly as possible and trying to correlate these images with identifiable features. The spot he was when I drew looked tantalizingly close and I felt sick I hadn't taken the fraction of a second longer necessary to ensure an accurate shot.

There was no telling when Mack would get the message, if he got it. The hurricanes had damaged many of the cells and communication by cell phone was spotty and aggravating and my phone seldom worked. The wound was unquestionably mortal and with the landmarks from my elevated view from the stand as aids, I renewed and redoubled my efforts to find a trail or sign. Exhausting this effort, I began patterning the acres and acres of gallberries, scanning for a hint of the buck or of blood. Stymied in this as well, I followed the edge of the cypress. The forbidding nature of the deep water and the piled debris from the storms made it seem unlikely he entered it, but of course, if there was an easy way in he would know it and a mature buck might readily resort to seemingly impenetrable places. Still, in more than four hundred yards of edge, no place showed sign of his passage. Back out in the palmettos and gallberries, wading through the thick, I searched with diminishing optimism. Darkness fell. Back at the truck there was no word from Mack.

The next morning, I resumed the search. Our deer have a great enough surface area to volume ratio to cool fairly quickly and have little to no fat to spoil so, on the occasions we end up recovering them the next day the venison is still fit and fine. With no blood, I resolved to cover as much territory as possible, cognizant that he could have slipped through the relatively narrow cypress strand and into the vast amount of overgrown pasture that lay west of it, but decided to limit my efforts, at least for the time being, to the area east of the strand because the way he raced off at an urgent and sustained flying pace, unlike a gut shot animal, gave hope that he hadn't traveled excessively far and that he hadn't attempted the arduous ordeal of swimming where logs and branches and trees blocked every avenue. In addition, no evidence of an animal entering the strand had been apparent the night before. I trod about for an hour, then two, pushing further and further south, gradually losing any lingering confidence and finding it difficult to even maintain hope. My thoughts turned to buzzards and, with my next chance to return being four days distant, I wondered if the scavengers would still gather then in numbers large enough to reveal the buck's remains and manifest where I should have looked.

A soft splooshing sound stopped me and I discovered a big, black boar hog six yards ahead in the thick, puddled pasture. I nocked an arrow and with no sign of nervousness pulled Bane Too back deeply and let a perfectly aimed arrow fly which drove through the hog's chest. He busted through the brush exploding into and through the densest vegetation and, showing the toughness and hardy vitality of big boars, made it nearly one hundred and fifty yards before expiring, but leaving a heavy, red trail in his wake. I followed easily, hampered only by the chokingly thick growth, each step along the reddened path a taunting example of the trail I should have had for the buck had I only been more careful with my shot.

The boar was huge, probably two hundred pounds. I'll never know for certain because with my recent back surgery and the absolute failure of my first attempts to drag him, I butchered him there and began toting the meat, anticipating two trips. With the first load I headed directly toward my stand as it would then allow me access to the trail to my truck. The stand was my north bearing during the grids I walked the night before. When after a hundred or so yards, even though my expectations of finding sign of the buck had now ebbed nearly away, I happened upon a spot I recognized and knowing the line from there standward had been searched, it seemed prudent to sidestep ten or so yards with my burden of meat and then renew my trek toward the stand and thereby ensure a scan of different terrain. A step or two after the jog, a brown object, an old log or branch showed vaguely five feet ahead through the thick forest of gallberries. "Wouldn't it be great if that was my buck?" I said to myself without hope or enthusiasm, but another step manifested that it was the case! Unbelievable! In all this thick growth, I had stumbled upon him and had walked within at least ten yards of him the evening before.

He was a nine point, his rack beautiful and dark and I wondered if he was the buck I encountered on opening morning, the morning of the day of the second hurricane. My journal notes describe him, "....and sure enough a beautiful buck followed about ten minutes later, his coat tawny and even, his antlers so distinct from his head it was as if he were wearing them rather than carrying something that was part of him. They were rich, deep, bronze and the dew had them gleaming as though they had been dipped in teak oil and burnished to a deep shine."

My plans for a two trip tote vanished and the idea of the extra work only made my smile broader. By the way, back at the truck my phone held a message from Mack offering his and Skylar's aid.

3

Some Airy Hunts

Olfaction is, as hunters know, a deer's most trusted sense. A peculiar sight or movement may cause a deer to flee, but as often as not the deer may bob its head to adjust its view or stamp its hoof. Likewise, an unnatural sound might cause a deer to circle downwind for confirmation, but it is rare indeed for a whitetail to seek confirmation upon encountering human scent. Therefore, the air and the movement of air factor critically into hunts.

There are sprays and washes and clothing available to minimize human scent, but I have yet to come across anything that completely eliminates it. Of course, Florida is a tough testing ground with its high humidity and very warm temperatures. In cooler climates much of a hunter's scent rises into the air to be carried away. That certainly is not typical here. Air warmer than its surroundings rises, but when the air temperature is not much different than body temperature, the air around a hunter and the scent it bears lifts little if at all. In addition, the high humidity not only increases one's perspiration and thereby the overall scent level, but at the same time enhances the olfactory ability of deer. Also, many scent reducing agents rely on carbon or another material adsorbing scent molecules which requires the molecule to come in contact with the scent reducing agent, but often I arrive at my stand with clothing completely saturated with sweat and dripping which severely restricts any molecule from reaching the carbon. While these products may be remarkably helpful in cool, dry conditions, the moist and hot air of Florida render them less effective.

A few episodes may illustrate how fitful and fickle the moisture rich air of Florida can be.

One morning found me in the misty air of the Bull Creek swamp woods. My stand was hung on the trunk of a tall cabbage palm and the fronds of a shorter one under it offered nearly perfect concealment. Although the day was sure to warm, it was still early and quite comfortable. Pileated woodpecker calls rolled through the damp forest and then one started drumming on a dead and hollow sounding tree. A shallow channel of the creek showed big, repeated ripples. Soon soft splashes accompanied my glimpses of brown, stilt-like legs. A large doe and a short antlered, but stockily built spike ambled up and fed under my stand for several minutes actually skirting around the trunk of my tree a couple times and then remained within forty yards for the next forty-five or more minutes with no evidence of them catching even a whiff of human scent. Their faces were similar and quite striking with distinct white spectacle-like patches around their eyes edged with thin, black rims. While they sniffed for water oak acorns and nibbled ferns and other green plants, an alligator crept down the creek, sliding in the wetter parts, walking in the shallows, and climbing over limbs and logs. His movements were stealthy and silent and amazingly produced next to no ripples.

He did not really seem large enough to prey on full-grown deer being no more than five and a half feet in length, but I was curious to see how the pair would react to this creature. Surprisingly, they either paid him no attention or failed to notice him and he continued on without pause.

Winds in the swamp are strange and this morning they had been steady, but quite light from the northwest. These deer, which had circled the base of my tree and fed in all directions around me including downwind for almost an hour, suddenly lifted their noses skyward and began acting cautious manifesting their detection of my scent. They did resume feeding, but only as they headed away and not in the same leisurely fashion.

Two light feathers are tied to my bow, one on each end and they help show the subtle and fickle nature of the air movement in the swamp woods. Sometimes, the two feathers do not point the same direction and they are only sixty inches apart. A little flour of sulfur or any of the light, wispy seeds I sometimes pocket and later release from my stand can dramatically demonstrate the tortuous routes the wind currents sometimes take through the trees, curving in many directions including up or downward. Seldom are these patterns stable and testing a few minutes later can give a drastically different picture.

Our bodies shed dead skin cells and the oils and bacteria that adhere to them continually and at a rate of hundreds of thousands per minute and these particles are the primary component of our scent trail. When the wind fluctuates and eddies swirl this way and that, the scent laden particles are being distributed about and can alarm or alert animals later even if the wind is steady and favorable then. Many hunters have told me of upwind deer suddenly becoming uneasy or cautious and I can't help but wonder if an eddy or an earlier eddy might not be the true explanation. Truly stable air flow around a stand in our swampwoods is an unusual occurrence.

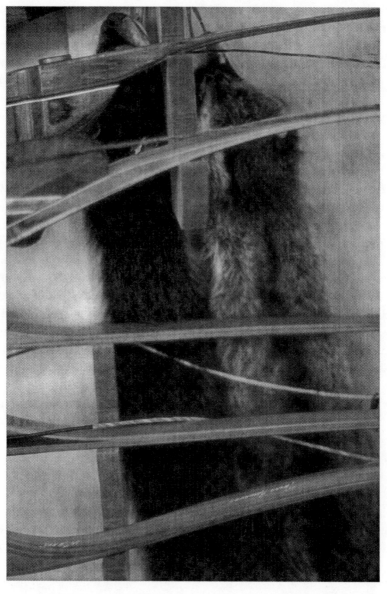

Melanistic raccoon skin nest to the skin of a normal raccoon.

Another morning in Bull Creek, not too far from the stand site in the previous account, I greeted the day. The wind had been steady from the southeast for a couple days and was forecast to remain so for a day to two more. The approach to the stand was easily accomplished in a flowing stream thereby minimizing my scent trail. The afternoon before with the same steady winds a five-point buck had fed close and never smelled me and I captured him on video. A blackish form worked down the creek moving raccoon-like, but colored like an otter. As it drew closer, I realized it was a melanistic raccoon, totally black. I arrowed it and have the tanned skin yet today. There is a small patch of dark, burnt orange fur near its tail and, on close inspection, the tail reveals darker bands, but otherwise it is midnight black, an incredibly beautiful skin. I've seen only one other melanistic raccoon to such an exaggerated extent and it was a kit. Its three litter mates were normal in color and I was lucky enough to video both color variations.

That evening nothing scented me and as this morning progressed, my luck held. Three does traipsed through ferns and sloughs to search for fallen acorns. Their teeth crunched each one they found loudly. Even though they were within a few yards, the largest one always seemed to be head on toward me and I desired a broadside or quartering off shot. Needless to say, three sets of nostrils in the swamp woods made me uneasy, but finally she was broadside with her head down. Concentration came without conscious thought and my recurve, Deer Bane, drove the silent, heavy arrow through her chest. She took an explosive leap, startling the other two deer, but stopped ten yards from my tree. Her knees buckled and she sunk upright to the ground, rolled to her side, kicked each foreleg once, and was dead. Her companions had not bolted far and lingered somewhat uneasily in the vicinity for a while.

The other two deer eventually left and with the wind still from the southeast I viewed two different deer sixty or more yards off. Then an exceptionally large doe approached from the northeast and I videoed her as she fed about within a few yards of my tree. She may have caught a faint trace of my scent when she passed downwind as she lifted her nose to sniff a few limbs and leaves, but she never became alarmed and, at last fed away.

A downy woodpecker came and hung upside-down on a vine and ate its berries and an otter swam upstream below my stand. Next, a tremendous buck, with a wide, heavy symmetrical eight point rack approached from the northeast taking the same approach as the doe. I videoed him as he was out of the ordinary, adorned with massive antlers with thick, tall tines. There would be plenty of time to shoot because his course was the same as the doe's. I traded video camera for bow when he drew within thirty yards. Suddenly, a hard gust of wind hit my back, filling me with alarm and dismay. Instantly, the buck's nose reached up and he loped off. The wind blew hard from the west for twenty minutes and then switched back and stayed out of the southeast for the rest of the day. A young rifle hunter killed this deer the next season and the rack it sported was not only the largest to come out of our hunting land that year, but also one of the best for the entire region. It was his first ever buck.

Another time in a different part of Bull Creek in the 'Throw Up Stand' (not named for how I hung it) with south winds, I waited on another remarkable buck I felt I had patterned. Two does slipped out of a muddy slough and then splashed down a clear, tea-colored creek directly below the south side of my stand. They were barely twenty yards past me when the buck emerged from the same slough and followed behind them. In less than a minute he would be broadside and scant feet away. His antlers gleamed in the subdued light of the swamp, a bony white with shadowed grey and chocolate bases. He was head on at no more than twenty yards when the wind issued from the east-north-east and the next second he was gone. This wind lasted five or ten minutes and faded back to south. Then another doe and fawn also came from the slough and plodded by me in the creek channel never sensing my presence.

These episodes convey how undependable air currents can be and the frustration of being betrayed by them despite one's best efforts. For me, these efforts include approaching the stand site from downwind or in flowing creeks in order to have clues to my presence in the fewest possible places. Even flowing water leaves somewhat of a scent trail washed along the edges as has been made plain to me repeatedly by otters following another otter at a fast pace even when the first otter passed thirty or more minutes earlier. The pursuing otter sniffs along the shoreline for confirmation of the route at each of the many forks and branches of the stream barely slowing and invariably takes the appropriate branch or discovers the lack of scent and corrects almost immediately. This demonstrates just how impossible it is to leave no chemical traces in our paths, but flowing water does remove and minimize human scent better than stagnant water where the skin oils float and spread on the surface. Chapter 14 delves into this topic in greater detail.

Many young cypress trees had been rubbed along a fenceline that bordered a cypress pond and I had earlier placed a ladder stand against the largest sapling which was maybe three and a half inches in diameter at the level of the platform and no taller than the head of someone standing on the stand. The tree alone could not support the stand and required guy-lines rigged out to the bases of several other small trees.

The cypress pond was deep, but well used and easy trails ran to the stand on each side of the fence from either east or west. A heavily overgrown pasture of gallberries, saw palmettos, and briars sprawled on the south side of these trails to some distant cypress domes. In the predawn blackness, the air was heavily damp and the vegetation slick and dripping with dew. The weather radio reported current winds from the northwest and predicted winds to continue from the northwest for the day so, pushing my way through the tangled and resistant vegetation, I made my way to the stand from the southeast. My clothes were soaked immediately and better described as drenched by the time I reached the stand. The open trails parallel to the fence would have been much easier and drier, but knowing the region to the southeast would be contaminated with my scent by the action of the wind, I did not want to leave my scent trail on any other approach and thereby reduce the directions a deer could draw near unaware and at ease.

Early light revealed grey fog that gradually turned white and the particles of fog moved in mass in a slow, drifting tide to the southeast even though my sodden feathers hung limply. With the fading and dispersal of the night's blackness came the twitters of small birds in the surrounding shrubs and the rusty squawks of sandhill cranes settling into pastures through the mists and the raucous caws of crows preparing to abandon their roosts. The morning was by no means quiet and still yet the sounds in concert provided a sense of peacefulness and naturalness that I ruptured with loud clashes and grinds of my rattling antlers. The crows responded with an excited burst of frenzied caws, but then a stillness settled on the mist blanketed scape.

In less than two minutes, a buck approached on the trail from the west along the fence line. He was walking head up, brusquely and unhesitatingly and his path would take him broadside at four yards well before the northwest winds would carry any alarming scent molecules to him. His antlers were not wide and for a moment it seemed he was not a buck to shoot, but then I saw his tines and realized they were all long and daggerish and colored like raw honey. He was a beautiful eight point and Bane Too felt alive and eager in my hand as he strode deliberately on, now fifty yards, now forty, now twenty-five, leaving no time for me to become nervous. At twenty yards, however, he halted and raised his nostrils and I wondered idly if there was some scent on the brush he had encountered secure in my belief in the steady movement of the air to the southeast and only then noticing the tiny and individual elements of the fog were now sailing to the west. The buck spun on his hooves and streaked away. Instinct and Bane Too's limbs sped an arrow toward his fleeing form and it slipped under his chest as he leapt and even though it missed, I was again amazed to see how true it flew and how precisely, with no conscious awareness, one's mind could extrapolate a deer's course and speed and concurrently predict that of an arrow. Only the buck's vertical bound kept the two paths from intersecting perfectly. A close miss can offer some satisfaction and, on as difficult a target as a speedily bounding buck, I let the nearness of the streaking arrow assuage the vexation of the untimely fickle air currents.

That afternoon, after consulting the weather radio again which updated its predictions to a north-northwest wind, I set up on the northern tip of a skinny cypress finger of the far other side of the property and my feathers manifested the steady wind from the north-northwest for a few hours. Nothing seemed to be moving so I ventured a rattling sequence that was rewarded immediately by the appearance of an eight point.

His rack was wider than the morning's buck, but no heavier and the tines weren't nearly as long. The color of the rack was like the bark of a really old cypress tree. I see a rack of this color every couple years, although most of our bucks have antlers that are varying degrees of brown, from a deep rich root beer shade to walnut to even light amber. This one was grey like many of the mule deer in Colorado, but even lighter and the tips looked creamy.

He would head toward me from the north-northwest and then seem to lose interest and begin to feed. A couple tickling clacks of the antlers would encourage him to resume his course for a short while until some delectable plant caught his attention. After three more light, reminding rattles he was fifteen yards due west of me and heading so directly to my tree that it was not possible to predict whether he would pass north or south of it. Brush obscured his approach for the last twenty yards and then the cypress trunks were a barrier, but only for a moment, I thought.

As you have guessed, I was wrong. He stopped at fourteen yards and what little I could see of his body and posture through the small cypress trees gave evidence of an alert and nervous deer. I looked at my feather with disbelief. The wind was blowing unaccountably from the east for a second time that day and for both times to happen exactly when a nice buck was approaching steadily within twenty yards of me was unfathomable! The buck bolted abruptly without ever offering a shot and within a few minutes the wind tilted the Spanish moss to the southeast once more. An hour later the wind came from the east again, then from the southeast and stayed that way for the last half hour of light. No more deer came within sight.

Sometimes the air movements, as fickle as they are, contrive in some way to carry one's scent everywhere except to a deer. There is another spot I used to hunt quite a bit where a thin, wooded creek strand comes down from the north, turns to the west a hundred yards or so and joins a north-south creek woods, forming an upsidedown lower case 'h' from the air and the pastures that surround it, though thick with briars and myrtles, are treeless. My stand was placed in a scrub oak in the short east-west section so low that I could reach up and hang my bow on it from the ground. With the channels of pasture and the walls the creek woods formed the winds funneled and changed at will and whim, but it was amazing how often I was not detected.

Once a doe appeared from the thick pasture directly north of me, angled to my left and continued to circle behind me and to my right, completing three-quarters of a circle, continually within 20 yards of my stand and never acting nervous even though my indicating feathers were fluttering about. A second deer appeared where she had come from and walked toward her, to my right, with a posture more like a dog than a deer. He was a buck with huge bases; at least five, possibly six inches in circumference, but the bulbous antlers were not three inches long. His body was large.

She looked at him without moving. He bounded up to her, licked her tail and quickly climbed on her back. A few seconds later she launched forward three or four yards and then stood very still and hunched up with her tail up and out and her head low. She quivered there for four of five minutes then ran back toward the pasture. He wheeled after her and bred her again. They mated a third time before they left and never showed any sign of smelling me despite the wind winding around me like the hands of a clock and their paths in concert formed a complete circuit about the stand at close range.

Talking about air movement and winds brings up the question of deer movement in strong winds and I'm sure each area is different and probably many factors beside the winds themselves govern or at least influence how much movement will occur. My experiences have born out that deer are often nervous and jumpy in winds and understandably so with all the motion in their surroundings, but, nonetheless, I have often seen deer in times of high winds.

Once a minimal hurricane caught my dad and me out at the hunt camp. We were nearly forty miles from the coast and therefore not unduly alarmed. The power went out, of course, but the sustained winds never exceeded sixty-five miles an hour where we were. The storm's brunt hit during the predawn morning, but the first faint light showed nothing but grey, heavy, nearly horizontal rain. By 10:00 AM the rain was lighter and we decided to hunt. While my dad pulled on his boots out on the porch I surveyed the wildly bending trees and branches and was shocked to see a doe not far from camp screened by whipping dog fennels. I told my father that he might be able to make a close stalk in all the moving vegetation and he readied his bow while I followed with the video camera, sheltering it somewhat from the weather.

The winds were then probably no more than forty-five miles per hour, but so gusty that the movement of myrtles, fennels, and trees was extreme. The willows next to the pond were bent to the ground and the five foot dog fennels thrashed chaotically. Getting close to the doe was not too difficult and soon my dad drew his bow at less than ten yards. When he released the arrow, the violent fennels whipped again and knocked the flying shaft downward. The doe bounded off a few yards and crossed a raging torrent where dry sand had been the day before and then sauntered into a thick woods. It had almost seemed too easy, but it was not to be.

There are also days remarkable for their lack of wind and a description of a few hunts with little or no wind may be worthwhile to illuminate a bit of the nature of our swamps, marshes, and woods. From a stand in a piney woods, I watched a markedly uneventful morning. Few birds and no game animals had stirred and my feathers hung like plumb-bobs. About 8:15 AM a slow, whitish speck drifted eastward maybe thirty yards from me. Another showed and then another. Soon the air was full of them, all drifting in slow motion to the east. I discovered they were ants of some sort with extremely fragile and transparent wings. Even though my indicating feathers did not stir, there must have been a faint movement of air for the multitude of tiny, ephemeral beings drifted gradually to the east as a whole and later to the south. It was a strange picture, the silent and damp piney woods filled with millions of buoyant and unsubstantial snowflake-like shapes. The spectacle lasted perhaps twenty or thirty minutes and then the numbers diminished until only an occasional speck could be seen.

The sun was setting over the St. Johns' River marsh where the land is flat as far as the eye can see. The vegetation obscured all traces of water and always reminded me of Conrad Richter's book Sea of Grass, looking all even and level except where the wind would ripple it into subtle moving contours, but this evening there was no wind. The temperature was dropping with the sun. The sky was wonderful, clear, and dry, blue like a robin's egg, but not so pale, somehow more crystalline and deep. Half sunken, the sun was a fiery neon and two thin hints of clouds reflected the vibrant orange, gilding it with hot silver. Above the flat, far reaching sea of grass, accentuating the level horizon was a narrow band of very distant magenta.

The scene was striking, but the peculiar thing was the wisps. At first, I thought they were a multitude of little columns of vertical smoke rising lightly in the still air spread here and there over the entire vastness of the marsh or maybe vertical puffs of mist or fog, but I discovered they were dense swarms of some insects, their tiny bodies silhouetted and their wings, silvery in the reddish sunlight imparted the misty appearance. Each column was a vortex only three to six inches in width yet close to four feet high and, while the individuals were no doubt moving rapidly, the swarm was stationary and quite pleasing to behold. The rarefied pillars were scattered about at distances of ten to thirty yards and extended over the whole flood plain. Each swarm hovered above a particular branch or leaf starting about a half foot above it and rising in a narrow, silvery wisp.

It was an odd and breathtaking sight especially in concert with the crystal blue dome of the sky, the still, cool air, and the red orb of the sun. The number of tiny creatures to put on such a show, dancing over the vast sea of marsh is unimaginable. Although this probably was not unusual for nature, I had never witnessed it before nor have I since.

In harmony with a discussion of light winds, an excerpt directly from one of my journals might fit well here to conclude this chapter:

"Like many archery season mornings, a layer of fog lay heavily over the pasture this morning in a thick, white blanket. Even before the sky lightened at all, the whiteness that enveloped the land was visible and everything was quiet and serene. With the gradual brightening of the heavens, cypress domes and bayheads became visible; steep, dark islands projecting above the sea of white in a soft, hushed world.

Most of the fog was flat and level, a white, ethereal strata. Here and there, the upper portions of taller myrtles could be seen, the level fog hiding the remainder like a vapory, insubstantial version of a lake of flooded timber. There was wind, too, light and unsure of itself, blowing from the north momentarily and deciding minutes later to ease out of the southwest.

West from the stand that offered me this otherworldly view, was a pond fringed with thick myrtles and the fog on all sides of it lay as I've described, flat and level, but over the pond the fog formed a dome-shaped hump attaining easily three or four times the height of the rest of the fog when the wind was still. When the wind breathed gently one way or another, the hump would break apart and pieces of it would drift ghost-like over the pasture, silent wraiths fading to nothingness.

The shifting winds and limited view were not advantageous to bowhunting, but they so typified our Florida early morning hunts and doused the land with the clean whiteness of a new day that I could not help but be moved to appreciate them. Such a morning holds a feeling, the essence of our woods and it seemed I was breathing in the very soul of nature.

As these thoughts and the appreciation of this wild, lonely scene coursed through my mind, a bobcat stepped through a clump of myrtles no more than ten yards away. He arrived silently, turned his whiskered face both directions to survey the small open area and padded away spirit-like. No sound heralded his presence, nor his departure as his greyish brown fur grew soft and hazy and then disappeared into the fog. He was gone and I thought if this morning held the essence of our woods and wildlands, what could better capture the spirit of this morning than this large tom bobcat, a ghost-like hunter, drifting silently out of and back into the mists?

The sun climbed skyward and the sunrise, always a pretty and welcome sight, was not an especially breath-taking one. However, the fresh rays of the sun did two things to make the foggy, misty morning even more striking. Dew had drenched everything and now the sun rays illuminated a myriad of crystalline droplets so that they glistened and glittered everywhere, painting myrtle leaves, pine needles, spider webs, and cypress leaves a shimmering, shining liquid silver. Where beams fell between the shadowy trunks of cypress trees, the fog took on a fiery hue.

A movement revealed the head of a whitetail buck peering around the shadowy side of a myrtle. Behind him were the slowly floating mists and he himself looked no less vapory and insubstantial. His head thrust forward a little more and sunlight caught the amber bones of his rack and it now looked hard, solid and real. There were nine points, yet the rack was still symmetrical, one beam merely hosting an extra tine near its tip. The tines were not exceptionally long, but the rack had heavy, bony mass that it carried throughout the entirety of its beams and even into the tines themselves. The antlers had impressive spread as well and the dew-wetted points gleamed a shiny yellow in the sun rays with dark undersides and brown bases.

He moved among the myrtles and disappeared and ten minutes elapsed before I found him again. A cautious buck, he took few steps without first exercising his eyes, ears, and nose maximally. In a half an hour he covered maybe forty yards at a diagonal which brought him only slightly closer to my stand. During that time he melted into and out of view not unlike the mists rising from the pond. Even knowing he was there, much of the time I could not find him and I had binoculars to aid my search.

The buck left without coming near enough to hear the flight of an arrow or a song from my bow. No sound had he made and he moved as if he floated on the mists. He embodied the spirit of the misty, mysterious, wild Florida morning best of all".

My journal entry thus ended, but it reminded me of one short observation I might include here. The sun rose on another morning of dense fog and I was amazed to witness a large, vivid circle colored like a rainbow against a cypress head across from my stand. It appeared to surround a shadowy center almost as if it were a giant halo of vibrant reds, blues, greens, yellow, and purple. It was striking and discreet and several minutes passed before I realized the grey at its center was actually my shadow and later I learned this phenomenon is called a Brocken Specter.

4

The Chestnut Buck

Don, a friend of mine, was keen for a chance at a deer or hog with his longbow so one day in archery season we went to a big oak scrub we call the Peanut Field. With its multitude of acorns which ripen before the larger water oaks and live oaks, it is a bow season game magnet. That morning, however, the animals moved little or not at all and if I remember correctly, between the two of us we saw a grand total of zero deer and hogs. We may have spotted a turkey or two.

With a business meeting scheduled for the afternoon, Don needed to leave by 12:30 so we had agreed to meet back at my truck at 11:00 AM to provide a little time for trailing and cleaning game in case his luck had been good. With nothing to trail or dress there was a little time left to continue the hunt and Don, as always, was enthusiastic and not one to squander a minute of the day so we drove through some pastures scanning for hogs and taking a circuitous route toward where we had left his truck. With such a dearth of activity in the morning, it seemed possible game might be afoot during the mid-day and this proved true.

In a dry pond ringed by myrtles, briars and grapevine, I spied a group of twenty or so hogs. Don grabbed his bow and I snatched up the video camera and we set off to stalk them selecting separate routes. The pond fringe offered great stalking cover and soon we were amidst them, but out of each other's sight.

Apparently a sow was in heat and one large boar hog, black and heavily shoul-dered, was busy chasing lesser boars away. The air was full of angry grunts and submissive squeals. His demeanor was arrogant, aggressive, and vainglorious as he strode back and forth on patrol, lunging viciously and hooking his tusks at any boar which failed to give way before him. He didn't deign to notice the shoats and piglets and several times would have trampled over them bristling, proud, and vaunful had they not scooted squealingly out of his path. It made some nice video footage; my only regret is that in my attempt to show the other hogs as well, I wasn't directing the camera toward him at the time Don's arrow streaked over his back.

We followed the somewhat spooked hogs into a roundish cypress dome to the east. Inside was an unbelievably thick mass of luxuriant greenery. Tangles of greenbrier and other vines throughout the ferns, wiry grasses, bays and myrtles rendered passage slow and difficult at best, but what caught the eye was that nearly every cypress tree around the perimeter was blazed down to its yellow and orange sapwood. This was a good buck's core area.

We didn't get back on the hogs and after Don, still upbeat and irrepressible, left for his meeting, I scouted the area more fully. Most of the buck's sign was around the nearly impenetrable head, but some was further to the east across a north/south dike. The rest of the members of my hunt club use rifles when the general season starts and also my formative years bowhunting public land taught me the value of hunting thick areas with little to no view that other hunters would never consider, but during our archery season I prefer stand sites with a large viewing area because this is the time the bucks roam and also when they are most conducive to being called or stalked. They actually spend less time in their core areas during this long, drawn out rutting period and one sees many bucks by hunting doe rich areas. In the end, I had been seeing many other good bucks at other, easier to hunt places and meeting close opportunities so regularly that I decided not to take time away from them to pursue this deer.

By general gun season, my other spots weren't producing sightings as predictably and I set two stands along the dike, one south and one north of the head and sat on each one once. From the south one I saw three does that slipped through some gallberries perhaps twenty-five yards from the stand.

From the other stand I spied a small eight point. He came out of a large triangle of myrtles that extended north from the thick head and was feeding in an open pasture, eating something small, but plentiful which appeared to grow quite close to the ground. Getting down from the stand required stealthy and perfectly timed movements, but then the stalk became routine for seventy or so yards because of the cover palmettos offered. Unfortunately, the cover ended and he was still beyond comfortable bow range. The buck was completely in the open and seemed content to feed in that spot indefinitely having moved little since he arrived there twenty or more minutes earlier. I could see no other direction of approach that would take me closer and darkness was not too distant.

I used my mouth to imitate a young deer's grunt and he walked unhesitating toward me, alert and curious. At twenty or twenty-five yards he balked and another grunt failed to lure him closer. He turned broadside and I sent an arrow whisking by him. Maurice Thompson tells of how satisfying a near miss with an arrow can be and I can remember the same sense when, picking a flower or twig many yards distant, my arrow struck tantalizingly close, but a complete miss at a broadside buck at less than twenty-five yards didn't offer anything of the kind and, to make it more frustrating, it occurred during a period of many, many misses. Those misses, by the way, also explain why, when I earlier mentioned all my close opportunities on good bucks, I still had both my buck tags.

Ozzie was rifle hunting from a stand a hundred and fifty yards east of the dike and the next day he slew a nice buck. The rack was handsome, its only weakness lay in the brow tines which were tiny broken stubs and that defect wouldn't affect the flavor of its haunches so I was happy to see it hanging in our cooler.

Because of my sighting of a small buck, the deer Ozzie took from the general area, and my good fortune of finding sign and seeing bucks elsewhere, I neglected the area until one day I wanted one of the stands to hang in a different site. It had rained most of the night, but still several fresh sets of tracks from a giant deer were present. I took the stand down, but then scouted and found an abundance of sign on the edge of the dense cypress head again. A deer jumped from the thick growth and with great splashing leaps raced away southward unseen. The north perimeter of the head, sheltered by the dense triangle of myrtles, held many buck rubs and under one large one I discovered a big pile of dry, orange bark shavings. The previous night's rain hadn't diminished until nearly dawn.

This rub was where the cypress dome came closest to another, tiny cypress head that jutted to the north. The day I hung my stands along the dike, I had driven by this head and spotted a buck that had high-tailed instantly into the dense dome. The memory of that sighting coupled with the freshly shaved cypress sapling compelled me to hang a stand at the spot. As I brought the stand to the site I jumped a huge, grey buck from the myrtles that raced tail down with unbelievable speed to the thick dome.

In the foggy light of early morning the following day, a buck drifted ghost-like out of the tiny cypress head and across the pasture to disappear into the thick sea of myrtles to the east. I proffered a light grunt which he ignored. He was a tall deer with a long neck and his rack was not as large as the buck that rocketed from the myrtles the day before.

I tried the stand one evening a few days later. Woodstorks wheeled about and landed in the small cypress dome and just before dark, three does congealed magically near me and beelined to what I thought was a myrtle. In the fading light I watched them reach into the tree and feed, chewing and crunching loudly. This went on for twenty minutes on only the one tree and I concluded that there must be a small live oak in the myrtles that somehow I had overlooked. The noisy chomping and crunching could then be attributed to acorns. I had remained in my tree because of an extreme reluctance to frighten deer from an area I planned to hunt again, but by now it was too dark to see anything. Waiting five minutes past the last crunching sounds, I started to climb down. The does turned out to be only twenty yards away and blew repeatedly as they spooked.

Overcome with curiosity, I investigated the small tree by flashlight beam and learned it was a myrtle loaded with waxy, hard berries and that is what the deer were eating. The other nearby myrtles had no berries. I have been around countless myrtles, before this episode and since, and never witnessed such enthusiastic and extended feeding despite plenty of these berries being present. Of all times to see this feeding behavior, this particular fall demonstrated one of our heaviest mast crops with acorns, persimmons, gallberries, and cabbage palm berries incredibly abundant.

Between unfavorable winds for the stand and the lure of swamp hunting, weeks passed without me returning. The swamp woods always beckons me, especially when the water oaks are dropping acorns because the abundance of life and activity is riveting and keeps both my attention up and expectations high. A good buck could happen along, but for a big buck chances are better near cypress and bayheads. The trouble with these heads is that you can spend many hunts there without seeing anything. On the other hand, the swamp is always vital; otters frolic, hogs abound, does, raccoons, young bucks, squirrels, owls, merlins, ibises, 'gators, herons, wood ducks, bobcats, kingfishers, woodpeckers and more provide entertainment and education during the long vigils.

On a cold, rainy day in late December I managed to get to our main gate about 5:00PM. Darkness would arrive about 6:00. I needed a close-by stand and the northwind was perfect for the one on the rubs. I managed to change clothes and clamber into the stand by 5:15. With the rain, I carried neither video recorder or camera and I have since wished fervently I had. Within seconds of some light rattling a grey deer appeared in the pasture. His rack was colored like oak bark and he had lots of whitish, short tines.

He was thirty yards out and broadside, but I didn't have the confidence to attempt that long of a shot and I believed once he was behind some myrtles, a few tickles of my antlers would tease him unbelievably close. The wind was ideal and it would be nearly impossible for him to circle downward. I was wrong. He was obviously curious for he recrossed the pasture, but this time 45 yards out looking several times in my general direction, but never venturing any closer. He disappeared into the myrtles at the same spot the early morning buck had gone.

The big triangular myrtle thicket contained a pond dense with dried vegetation at this point and it appeared the bucks were using the myrtle fringe as a corridor to and from the tangled head. There were no trees to hang a stand nor low level visibility for a ground blind, but three days later the forecast was right and I moved a homemade tripod to the spot and embedded it in a thick clump of myrtles. It disappeared and anyone standing on it should be nearly invisible as well.

I sat there that evening, but not with a great deal of confidence. The myrtles made it impossible to shoot except in a few scattered places that were quite close to the stand and the trouble would be seeing the buck coming in time to take advantage of these limited shooting lanes. The exception, of course, was the open pasture to the west, but it was less likely a deer would come from there this late in rifle season. This lack of confidence degraded into misgivings about my choice of hunting areas when my feather showed that the wind, predicted to be from the south, was actually west-south-west and the cypress head was blocking enough of it to cause a suck-back toward it so that my scent was being spread about 190 degrees. I had spent the mid-day placing two other stands in addition to this tripod and each spot showed promise. If time was not so short, I would have moved, as discouraged as I felt then, but walking to the truck, driving elsewhere, and subsequently walking to a stand would involve too much of a short winter afternoon.

Then, in the day's last hour, the wind lightened dramatically. Usually when the wind diminishes, it becomes more fickle, but this time it steadied and carried my scent only to the northeast. I smiled contentedly and resolved to enjoy this evening. Three distant deer, at least two of which were does, scudded like brown streaks across the pasture to the southwest. The pasture was extremely open there except for some patches of high grass and short myrtles and apparently they were bedded in some such unsuspected cover, but upon rising had no desire to linger in the open.

A tiny sound emanated from the east near the edge of the cypress. It was minuscule and I would have ignored it if it hadn't been repeated a few minutes later from the same spot. Other than a few buzzards that winged overhead and the group of running deer, I had seen no animals so I searched clumps of grass with binoculars for the noise's source guessing a mouse was stirring in one. I found a motionless brown leg. There was a buck fifteen yards off. He was short, thick necked, and chestnut brown. His antlers were regal; rust colored below with the long tines lightening to amber with ivory tips.

Despite his nearness, he was head on and every traditional bowhunter knows how risky that shot is. This buck was phenomenally cautious, bending down to pull some small leaf from the grassy ground and then looking about for minutes before another nibble. He was even more alert and vigilant before or after any step. He was able to remain still for extended periods with no swiveling or cocking of ears, swishing of tail, wiggling of nostrils, or chewing. I have never seen a doe behave this way, but several times I've watched bucks as extraordinarily cautious as this one.

Eventually, he stepped closer, but instead of providing a more favorable target, the step only sheltered him behind a myrtle. Although he was hard to make out through its branches, he would have no difficulty detecting any movement of my skylighted silhouette so I endured the gathering mosquitoes. He continued to move little, eat little, and scan about a great deal and this was in very thick cover. Fifteen more minutes passed before he covered the six yards that brought him broadside, ten yards off with no interfering vegetation. Any hunter reading this is sure to realize how long my heart was pounding for it started with my first glimpse of his leg, how often I held my breath as his head searched for danger, the nervousness of being this close and knowing the chance can vanish in a millisecond. Now it seemed my opportunity was at hand and my heart hammered even harder.

As I drew, he looked up, maybe catching my furtive movement or maybe just out of wariness like all the other times he had scanned the area. I couldn't be sure, but I wanted to let the arrow fly from three quarters draw and had to exert my willpower to force myself to draw Deer Bane another three or four inches. Then, finally feeling the broadhead with my finger, I fervently hoped my feel for the aim was true. Up to this point things had happened at an agonizingly slow pace, but now it was the opposite and was over in a rapid blur; the bright fletches leaping from the bow, the nearly simultaneous muffled thud of the bow and the hard 'crick' of the striking broadhead, and the instant collapse of the buck!

He was an absolutely beautiful buck. His antlers held eight long, graceful tines and the symmetry was perfect. He was not particularly heavy and his kidneys had no fat about them at all. This is probably due to his involvement in rutting activities, but judging from what I saw, could be attributed to how slowly and how little he ate! Kidding aside, it could have been related to his inability to eat for his lower left third molar was fractured, the facial half missing and the remainder was loose in the jaw and obviously abscessed.

5

Florida Bowhunters

"So long as the new moon returns in heaven a bent, beautiful bow, so long will the fascination of archery keep hold of the hearts of men."

Most bowhunters are familiar with this quote and with Maurice and Will Thompson because of Maurice's book <u>The Witchery of Archery</u>. These brothers wrote of archery shortly after the Civil War for many of the outdoor periodicals of their day reminding all of the romance and beauty of the bow and popularizing bowhunting. Their deep love of archery and nature shines through their literary works. Most of their adventures occurred in Florida and, therefore, our swamplands served as the birthplace of modern bowhunting. Beautiful verbal portraits of these wildlands spring forth from their articles and books.

The war impoverished them in circumstance and health and in its aftermath they were disallowed firearms. The difficulties and troubles of the giant events that shaped their early lives did not daunt the young men who went on to become authors and attorneys and to enjoy wildwood adventure with bows and arrows. Many people attribute the Thompson's love of bowhunting to their lack of firearms, but in truth, they bowhunted even as youngsters.

Pope and Young are familiar names to all bowmen and some perspective of the Thompsons' contribution to archery and bowhunting might best be conveyed by quoting Saxton Pope: "To Will and Maurice Thompson we owe a debt of gratitude hard to pay. The tale of their sylvan exploits in the everglades of Florida has a charm that borders on the fay. We who shoot the bow today are children of their fantasy, offspring of their magic. As parents of American archery, we offer them homage and honor."

Both Maurice and Will were gifted artisans with pen and paper and to introduce you to the heart and soul of these archers an excerpt from Will's writing late in life may serve best: "I would give almost any precious thing I hold to fare with you once to the game land of your choice, and to watch and wait by a slender trail while you and your young, strong comrades stole the secret haunts of the wild things, and to listen to the faint footfalls of the coming deer, roused by your entrance into their secret lairs. To see the soft and devious approach of the wary thing; to see the lifted light head turned sharply back toward the evil that roused it from its bed of ferns; to feel the strong bow tightening in my hand as the thin, hard string comes back; to feel the leap of the loosened cord, the jar of the bow, and see the long streak of the going shaft, and hear the almost sickening 'chuck' of the stabbing arrow. No one can know how I have loved the woods, the streams, the trails of the wild, the ways of the things of slender limbs, of fine nose, of great eager ears, of mild wary eyes, and of vague and half-revealed forms and colors."

One last excerpt from Maurice is worth including and, if you're like me, you may find yourself envying their vacation schedule.

"How dreary a thing it is to come back to the humdrum and vexation of business life after four months of freedom, and all the charms of wild camp-life in such a region as Florida! For a time one is restless, and champs the bits of restraint, but all is for the best and eight months will soon run by. They have run by again and again, and Will and I have drawn the bow on spots in Florida where never a white man fired a gun. Our steel arrow-heads will be found imbedded in the trees of those strange forests a hundred years from now."

Although I have yet to find any of their arrowheads, I've buried more than a few of my own in tree trunks mayhaps in the very same forests that harbor theirs.

Undeniably, the Thompsons pioneered modern bowhunting, but it is no secret that there were bowhunters in our swamplands long before their time. Although Howard Hill came later, his descriptions of Charlie Snow, a Seminole, may give some insight into the native hunters of the past. Here are a few quotes from Howard:

"…and I was amazed by his knowledge of game and stalking. He literally spoke the language of the animals in the Everglades of Florida. He could lure a turkey gobbler from the brush with the skill of the turkey hen herself, and I have seen him call bobwhites so close we could have caught them with a dip net. A bull alligator would come to the surface at Charlie's croak just as a baby guinea will dive for cover at its mother's signal. Bobcats, raccoons, and even muskrats, could be fooled by this Indian.

"When it came to stalking game, tracking animals, and knowing their habits, this giant Seminole of over six feet three inches was amazing. I have actually seen Charlie Snow track a rabbit in the grass, and anyone who doesn't think this feat calls for a finished tracker, should try it sometime. In a casual walk through forest everglade or woodland trail, nothing seemed to escape this man's alert eye. He could see farther and hear better than any other man I ever knew, and his judging of animal traits was a revelation."

No doubt the shooting methods and ranges of natives in the diverse habitats of America varied, but Howard's description and explanation of the Seminole's archery is intriguing:

"Those who have the conception that no American Indian can shoot a bow successfully in competition with the white man are simply mistaken. At close-range shooting Charlie Snow could make any white man I have seen or hunted with look like a novice. I readily admit his inefficiency at shooting at the longer ranges, but this is accounted for when one understands that the draw, or loose, of the Seminole is such that it is impossible for him to pull a heavy bow. With the light bow he uses, long-range shooting is made very difficult by the high trajectory of the arrow.

"As an example of Charlie's accuracy at close rang, I have seen him drop a corn cob on the ground ten feet away and begin shooting. He would break the cob in half, break the halves into fourths, the fourths into eighths. When he had finished, there would be no piece of the cob larger than the end of a man's thumb within twenty yards. His amazing accuracy would still hold up to twenty-five yards, but above that range Charlie had no desire to shoot, and refused to do so.

"When one studies the Indian's habit of living and his environment before it was disturbed by the white man, it is easily understood why these men didn't develop into longer-range shots. In the first place, the amount of game in most localities was plentiful, the brush thick enough to offer sufficient cover, and the absence of loud explosions such as are caused by firearms made the game less nervous and wary than now.

"Why shoot a rabbit at forty yards when by careful stalking the hunter can get within ten? Or why shoot a deer at sixty yards when, if one has the ability, he can get within fifteen yards? That seems to be the Indian psychology and to me it is certainly a sensible one, because Charlie proved to me many times that these feats of stalking were entirely possible even in this day and age of civilization and firearms."

Speaking of Howard Hill, a monumental figure in the modern history of bows and arrows, he began and developed his love of bowhunting in Florida. Not only did he learn the art of stalking and getting within close range of game from Charlie Snow, but he rode horseback over cattle pastures at night after hounds in pursuit of foxes and bobcats with his longbow, obviously an exhilarating yet almost reckless sport. His own words reveal his regard for Florida's swampwoods:

"No section of America affords the archer more opportunities for hunting than do the Everglades and sub-Everglades of central and southern Florida. There is not much big game, but the variety of lesser animals and game birds will give an archer more action in a day's hunt than any other place I have ever seen.

"Most people's conception of the Everglades, I have found, is not true to the country as it really is. Instead of huge forests of giant trees, it is made up mainly of vast meadows of switch grass and square miles of scrub-palm plains, interspersed with sawgrass, clumps of elbow bushes, and small cabbage-palm hummocks—or "hammocks," as they are called colloquially in south Florida. Of course, there are also some big cypress swamps that ring true to the average person's conception of the Florida Everglades.

"But don't feel that the lack of timber is a discouragement to the wildlife that abounds in numerous parts. Alligator, bobcat, cougar, fox, rabbit, deer, and many other animals often frequent this country far removed from the big cypress."

Obviously, Fred Bear should be included here as well. He promoted and advanced bowhunting in his day as much as the Thompsons, Saxton Pope, Art Young, or Howard Hill did in theirs. Fred enjoyed wintering here and ended up moving his archery equipment manufacturing operation to Florida and residing in the state for many years. The Fred Bear Archery Museum is adjacent to the plant and a place of wonder and enchantment for any lover of archery. Hours of entertainment can be had wandering amid the bows; some ancient, some beautifully artistic, and some peculiar and novel. In addition, on display are tidbits and glimpses of Fred's life.

Our swamplands have furnished bowhunting excitement for many great archers. The friends this book will introduce to you, Mack, Ozzie, my dad, Don, and Don may not be as famous, but have no less enthusiasm and love of the sport and a bit of preliminary information will further your acquaintance.

Ozzie and I have hunted together for nearly three decades, sharing long rides to distant hunt sites, applying for any special hunts we could, finding hidden niches in public management lands, sojourning out west, and eventually joining the same hunt club. Wherever he is, on public or private land, he nearly invariably comes out of the woods with some sort of trash or litter he has found and picked up. Knowledge that his efforts are virtually insignificant in the face of widespread carelessness and litter, does not daunt him from trying to keep the woods pristine. Ozzie generally chooses the most lethal legal weapon permitted by law and I have no hope of converting him to a traditional bow, but the love of the hunt and the wilds springs from deep within him, pleasantly affecting and cheering all in his company.

Mack is the most natural hunter I've met. Even when he first started stalking hogs, his movement was always perfect. So often hunters tarry when they should move, especially when air currents are whimsical, or move precisely when they should hold tight, but Mack's instinct is always on and this is true with deer and elk as well as underwater with grouper, cobia, and lobster. Hunting hogs by stalking to within a spear length is incredibly challenging when undertaken alone. Add another hunter to the mix and the prospects plummet. However, Mack and I have successfully speared hogs together on a few occasions. He is good company on any hunt regardless of difficulties or work involved. As mentioned elsewhere, his skills with his longbows and recurves are impressive.

My dad, Jim Lewis, began bowhunting when he turned 65 and I'll always be grateful to Florida's game commission for offering free hunting licenses for its seniors because that incentive initiated his first tastes of the sport. He had not hunted at all in a quarter of a century or more and had never hunted with a bow, but the privilege of a senior license prompted him to join my bowhunting forays. Before long we would enjoy archery shoots, apply for special hunts, scout deer all year 'round, and camp together for hunting weekends. When I joined the hunt club, he was my steady companion nearly every week and we shared untold hours and adventures in the swampwoods. His excitement and alacrity to hunt were always peaked and, like a youngster before his birthday, he would find sleep elusive before opening day. We were able to be part of one another's hunting successes which was special, but even more special, in my mind, are the memories of sipping hot cups of coffee, of quiet words as the truck's headlights cut the blackness of the predawn sky and then seeing the flood of stars as we stopped to open a gate, of meals together, and of a short games of cards before turning in for the night.

The two Dons are quite different, but parallel each other in both hunting only with traditional bows, both having impeccable integrity, and both brimming with passion for the sport. One, Don D. is a prankster and keeps camp life entertaining while the other, Don G., outgoing and warmly friendly, is more serious. Don D. abhors hogs while Don G. enjoys pursuing hogs nearly as much as whitetails. Both have furnished me good companionship, shared many adventures throughout the years, and enriched my hunting experiences.

6

Peculiar Hunts and Episodes

Two unusual episodes occurred one opening weekend of archery season. If one of the guys at camp told of the same experiences, I would reason that they were fond of telling good stories and appreciate it as such, but these events did happen and on successive days of the hunt. My arrows precipitated both events.

I was in my little homemade tripod in a small, stunted forest of oak scrub with an open pasture about me that sported a few other patches of scrub here and there. A big, dark, long-bearded gobbler came running at full speed from another patch and headed directly toward me. The stand was somewhat hidden, but not to a turkey's eye so I expected him to turn or fly any second, but he approached closer and closer without changing course! 150 yards, 100, 50, 30! Now he was in some low, scattered scrub and while I was shielded from his eyes I readied Moon Sliver. I assumed he would slow down having achieved the cover of the scrub, but he did not and his course would take him through an opening of about four feet that was twelve yards from the tripod before he reached the thick part of the scrub and was thereby protected from my arrows. When he reached the gap, I drew, led him a bit, and let go! The lead was too great and the arrow drove into the ground directly in front of him. His next stride brought each leg under the protruding portion of the shaft and tripped him! Down he went, not tumbling, but rather skimming on his belly and he lost not a second regaining his footing and racing away as quickly as he had come.

The following evening I slipped out of a big scrub to still hunt my way across a pasture to meet my dad. This pasture had been cut two or three years before and offered little cover. From the scrub's edge I could see three does chasing one another around this end of the pasture, scrambling about, stopping suddenly and even walking a step or two and then abruptly breaking into the chase again. Each time their course, as intermittent and unpredictable as it was, took them behind a palmetto patch, I would ease my way forward, crossing the fence and eventually into the pasture. As I was getting closer, their merriment, if indeed that is what it was, took them behind the one patch of scrub remaining in the pasture and I felt fate had smiled upon me and hurried forward to take full advantage of it. The clump would shelter my approach and offer good cover when I shot. However, they had not stopped behind it or even lingered. Barely obscured from my view, they wheeled back and caught me moving in the open. They all stopped and stared at me thirty yards off. The closest stamped her hoof. They all appeared the same size and were all adult.

I eased an arrow from the quiver, drew Moon Sliver, and focused on a spot. My arrow flew true, but, as readers who know whitetails will realize, quite futilely. By the time my arrow reached the spot, all three does were in flight and the one for which I aimed was at least eight or nine feet away! She landed with a deer's natural grace and bounded again. This time her front legs gave way as she came down and her chest plowed into the ground, her hind end somersaulting ahead and her neck bent back toward her now forward rump! It looked like her neck would be broken and the loudness and solidness of the thump when she hit emphasized the energy she absorbed. Even so, she was immediately back up and away keeping up with the other does, but emitting a high, short wheezing sound; a lot like a deer's alarm snort, but much shorter and sharper and higher and repeated, I believe, each time she breathed. Aih-aih-aih-aih-aih-aih-aih! I could picture if she had broken her neck and I brought her back to the camp without a hole in her and asked the guys what they thought about a shot like that!

In the same general area are some large pines scattered in a glade. From one such pine I could view the glade and a good bit of the scrub which was interesting because although it was beyond arrow range, the oaks that grew in the arid, sandy soil were dropping sweet, black acorns that attracted whitetails, wild hogs, and turkeys. The height of the oaks ranged from five or six feet to maybe sixteen feet and they filled an area of eighty acres, their dense branches interlocking except on the trails of white sand that laced through them like a complex maze. Clumps of palmetto were scattered here and there throughout the scrub and it was the sound of something crashing through their fronds that first attracted my attention. Although I could see over most of the scrub forest from my elevated perch, normally I could not see an animal unless it was within forty yards because, despite their stunted size, the oaks were taller then a deer's back and their foliage was too dense to see through. However, I spotted a flash of white tail in the direction of the sound and moments later a giant buck bounced into view in the same place.

I heard bits of the chase over the next few minutes and then the doe raced into the glade, turned and ran straight below me. What great luck! The buck immediately rounded the corner with hooves flying and spraying bits of the glade's grass and mud. He was almost under me. I drew my recurve, Deer Bane, led his chest and let fly! My arrow sped toward its target from point blank range, but, with the buck's head up and back, the broad head was intercepted by one of his heavy beams. Thwack! The arrow embedded in the bony antler with all the force and speed my bow could offer, but it seemed not to faze the thick set buck.

The doe stopped with the sound and when he saw her stop he drew up momentarily as well, but immediately launched after her anew and she bounded away. I could follow their progress because the vertical arrow with its pink fletchings protruding skyward from his antler extended above many of the trees of the scrub. Over the next ten minutes he chased her here and there on a circling, haphazard course and because the arrow, like a brightly colored antenna, kept me aware of their position, occasionally I could see flashes of one or the other of the pair. Despite my fervent hopes, they did not retrace their circuit through the pines and eventually I lost track of them as they entered the swamp woods.

In Florida, hogs are legal after dark and this fact has made me aware of something that otherwise would never have come to my attention. One October evening I sat in a stand on the outer edge of a cypress head overlooking a sandy dike and some scraggly pasture. I waited expectantly for I had set the stand up the previous day amid heavy deer sign and saw three that evening. In fact, a tall, lanky spike had sauntered up and remained within a few yards long enough that I had videoed some nice footage of him when he looked over his shoulder and walked back to the south. A doe approached and they rubbed or licked noses cautiously through a barb-wire fence after which she scatted back a few steps and then trotted north, crossed to my side of the fence and walked briskly away. He watched and then followed after her. This second evening I had yet to see a deer.

Perhaps twenty minutes before dark, a grand, coal-black boar bristled out of the thick head and fed on acorns in the open fifteen yards away. He was large and toothy and normally I would have tried for him, but I was so sure deer would arrive momentarily that I decided against it. Darkness fell however and I saw no deer. I could hear the hog move about, but his black bulk blended in with the shadows. Reluctant to spook him, I remained in the stand hoping he would soon wander off.

Finally it grew quiet under the oak and I readied myself and gear to climb down, but then I made out his dark form against some white sand directly below me and decided to shoot. Deer Bane drove an arrow through the backbone down into the chest, dropping the heavy boar on the spot. The remarkable thing was the sparky flash that occurred as the arrow first penetrated, like iron on flint. Despite the darkness, this flash brightly and distinctly manifested the point of entry of the arrow. I'm not sure if it is caused strictly by friction on the coarse hair or if sand and dirt in the hair is responsible.

Since that time, I've seen the spark on hogs a couple more times and I've spoken with two other bowhunters who have seen it. I am curious if it happens on the other game as well or is limited to the coarse, dirty, bristly hair of hogs.

One December morning, after a two hours of a period of lively animal activity when turkeys yelped incessantly, woodpeckers rolled tuneless calls through the swampwood, kingfishers fired their cries in staccato bursts, squirrels frolicked through the branches, and raccoons waddled with their hunched backs along the gently trickling creeks, the vigor ebbed suddenly from the forest and the swamp fell quiet and motionless. No birds twittered. No otters roiled the creek waters. I started writing and, undisturbed by movements or sounds, made good progress updating my journal.

About an hour and a half later, a glance to my left caught sight of a deer maybe one hundred yards distant. With time I determined there was a group of three does feeding in a wandering and haphazard fashion, but some of the movement was toward my stand. I tried to hold my hopes in check because there was no feature of the swamp to funnel them any certain direction and also because the wind, which had been steady from the north all morning, had become easterly in the past thirty minutes and these deer were not too north of west. A slight shift or gust in the wind could alarm them. Despite my concerns and doubts, they eventually approached and two were feeding thirty yards from my tree. Then one crossed Bull Creek and, only fifteen to eighteen yards distant, stood nearly downwind. Her nose came up suspiciously as I drew Deer Bane and urged myself to concentrate only on a bit of her coat. The shaft buried into her chest! There was no question as to the lethality of the shot and, sure enough, she tumbled within sixty yards.

The other deer, unsure what had transpired, stared nervously toward where she had dropped, their view of her fallen form impeded by the height of the ferns. They were still north of the stand and the wind held so they couldn't smell me. After several minutes, they blew and raced off only to come part way back and do it again. Even after I climbed down, pulled my stand, and made my way to the downed doe, they continued stamping and snorting. I took pictures of the doe in the creek bottom forest. My friends will all testify that my photographic techniques cannot be classified as quick. Then I bore the stand and my gear to the truck. I returned and skinned the doe's legs removing the bone and hooves, but leaving the dew claws to tie to opposite legs and thereby fashion a pack as described more fully in a later chapter. I shouldered her and carried her from the woods. Through all this, the other does had snorted, not with the loud alarm snorts they issue as they bound single-mindedly away, but with the more nervous ones that accompany their suspicions and their hoof stamping behavior. All told, they snorted for at least fifty minutes while I was present to hear and who knows how long they continued after my departure.

The doe weighed 95 pounds without her leg bones or hooves. Here is the curious part, but first a little history. The arrow that took my first elk penetrated only eight or ten inches into her lung and motion of the shoulder snapped off the shaft at this point. Upon dressing her, I learned that the short, broadhead tipped portion, worked its way out of the chest cavity completely and then somehow channeled forward grievously into the neck resulting in two distinct wound tunnels with only one hole through the skin. I could make no sense of this and I wrote in my journal at the time, "How this happened is difficult to conceive and I wonder if maybe the fatal nature of the wound was only some streak of bizarre misfortune for the elk and good luck for me." I now discovered a similar phenomenon with this doe. Being launched from an elevated position, the arrow cut through ribs and into the chest cavity and through the sternum yet did not cut through the skin under the chest. With her first or second bound, the nock end of the shaft broke off leaving a segment inside with the two bladed broadhead I used at the time. This section of the arrow backed out of the chest and subsequently drove forward outside of the ribs and deeply into her shoulder. Anyone who has tried to pull an arrow from a deer's chest which has cut through ribs is aware that it does not slide out easily and typically requires substantial force. I have no answer to this perplexing puzzle. I suppose the combination of chest compression during leaps, pressure in the chest cavity, and tugging by anything rubbing the protruding end of the broken shaft as the animal crashed through vegetation all acting in concert might explain the extrication of the arrow fragment, but it seems a flimsy explanation and then the forceful reintroduction down another pathway is still unexplained. The points in common are two bladed heads, chest wounds, broken shafts, and that the second wound channel extended forward. If it had happened only the one time, I wouldn't be so curious as any strange chain of events could have effectuated the result, but twice to a single bowhunter is less indicative of chance.

After a fairly uneventful hunt one December morning, I pulled my stand. As I trudged down the creek woods with the stand on my back, something fell with a heavy thud directly in front of me. At first, I guessed it to be a waterlogged section of an old limb, but the day was dry and the breeze scant. Peering through the thick shock of ferns, I descried a balled up yellow rat snake with two pinkish feet protruding between his coils. The feet were those of a flying squirrel. The body of the little creature was completely hidden although occasionally a glimpse flashed of its head and bulging eyes as the knotted amber and brown mass twisted and writhed. The feet twitched a couple times and the snake tightened its coils in response and threw another wrap around it. It is possible that the snake launched itself as its mouth grasped the squirrel or that upon grasping the little beast, the snake threw its coils about it without thought or concern about the fall. Less likely, the flying squirrel may have pushed off from the tree and carried the heavy serpent with it. Regardless, the snake seemed to have suffered nothing from the fall. Yellow rat snakes can climb nearly vertically up tree trunks with little or no obvious points of purchase in a nonchalant manner that appears at odds with gravity.

Many years ago, before I acquired a speedlight for my camera and was therefore subject to the difficulties of capturing crisp photographs of moving game below the canopy of the swampwoods with only the meager light that filtered through, a four point splashed down a slough twelve yards from my stand. I clicked a picture, but with a 200 mm lens and 1/15th second shutter speed, there was little chance of a successful result especially with a moving deer so I hoped for another chance with the buck stationary. The buck did stop, but behind an angled tree and was blocked from view. With patience I waited and was dismayed by his departing course which kept the trunk between us. Although he was too small to arrow, my commitment to trying for a photo was strong and I had not yet learned to limit deer calling to very restrictive circumstances. With my mouth, I grunted. He was forty or more yards distant and whirled around and loped back half that length, but still remained mostly obscured by vegetation. He searched and scanned a long while and then turned to leave. I grunted. He turned back, but soon turned away again. Each time he started off, I grunted and he would stop, but venture no closer and, in the end, he left despite my grunts.

A week or so later, he strode down the same slough while, from the same stand, I exposed a frame or two of film. Again convinced (correctly) that the pictures would be blurred, I endeavored to entice him back with a grunt. He looked up, but immediately resumed feeding and subsequent grunts elicited no response from him. There may have been a response, however, for a spike materialized quite close to my stand. When he reached the area of vegetation that shielded the four point from a picture in our prior encounter, the bigger buck saw him and approached him briskly with his hair erect and bristling. They sparred a brief minute or so and then the four point fed lazily toward the northwest. The spike stood without moving for well over five more minutes, head low and tail down, remaining that way even after the other buck was completely gone from sight. Eventually, the spike tip-toed timidly to a creek and drank, his posture still submissive and diffident. When he departed, it was to the east-southeast.

From a stand in a cabbage palm, I had watched the light change from diffuse and grey to sharp and hard and heard the red-shouldered hawks' ringing cries and the staccato calls of kingfishers, but had seen no game. Then plash! A pair of wood ducks set down in the main creek channel thirty yards from me. They headed north, but later swam back and continued south ignoring the small creek that veered from the channel to come within a few yards of my stand. It was screened by shrubs and vines that interlaced over it most of its short length, but was clear from above in direct proximity to my stand. For me, wood ducks were like turkeys; too sharp-eyed to offer very many chances at short range from a tree stand and while I had tried several times, I had yet to take one with a bow.

During the previous summer I had fashioned a wood duck call from a small piece of cow horn and I used this to imitate their sweet, shrill swimming call. Fallen logs and the luxuriant swamp growth hid them from view, but I was rewarded with an immediate reply. I called once or twice more and they swam back and floated and bobbed down my creek finger. When they emerged from the tangle of growth, the hen was in the lead, but I waited for the drake. When at last he cleared the over stream arbor, I let drive a shaft which whisked into the water contacting him by the merest graze or perhaps only as his momentum carried him against the vibrating quarrel. He jumped back a few feet and was thereby protected from a second arrow. The hen had stopped, too, but she was still in open water. With Deer Bane's next thunk, an arrow pierced her chest and, because of the shallowness of the water, pinned her so she could not fly, run, or swim. She fluttered about and then quieted and I assumed she would die momentarily. The drake did not leave, but I could find no unobstructed pathway for an arrow to reach him. I did not want to get down to retrieve arrows as I was buck hunting and loathed the idea of spreading my scent about and already my small quiver was diminished by two arrows.

However, it turned out I needed to get down for suddenly the hen had some-how dislodged the arrow from the bank and was swimming rapidly away up the deep, main creek. It happened so abruptly that, before I could react, she was gone. My first thought was that I could only wait and later walk the creek edges searching for her knowing it would take enormous good fortune to succeed, but then she swam back down the main creek and turned into a shallower finger north of me. This creek was wadable so I scuttled down from my stand.

When I reached the area, no trace of her was visible and I discovered many lit-tle interconnecting channels with the main creek. Had she returned to the deep water? The speed she swam with while burdened with an arrow was amazing. As I stood there, discouraged, a noise drew my attention back to the shallow finger. She was on the bank behind a log. I had arrived at the finger with an arrow ready on Deer Bane's string, but no sooner had I discerned her than she disappeared into the ferns. The trees and shrubby growth of the swamp woods prevented regaining any view. I had to wiggle under, over, and around a lot of branches and trunks and get quite close to try to achieve a shooting lane. Finally I could see the arrow, but as I raised my binoculars to determine where in the ferns she was posi-tioned, she ran off, pulling free of the arrow.

Now she was running quickly and I scurried after her trying to dodge limbs and circumnavigate young cabbage palms and fallen trees. If someone had been watching my antics and falls and scampering about, no doubt, they would have been hysterical with laughter, but I pursued her with earnestness knowing if I lost sight of her I would likely never find her.

A giant tree that appeared to be emerging from a mound with several smaller trees and a juvenile cabbage palm was in her path and I raced around it to prevent her from getting access back to the water. She did not come out. I went back to discover the mound was actually a large system of raised roots over which swamp debris and leaf litter had accumulated. There were several holes into it and prob-ing with my arrow revealed chambers that extended back several feet. After pok-ing about unsuccessfully for a bit from one side, I backed up to where I could stand and circled the cabbage palm. This spooked the hen from under a frond where she had been hiding and with dismay I saw her run into one of the little openings under the tree roots.

I broke off a long cabbage palm stem and used it to probe about. Portions of the chambers extended more than eight feet and on my hands and knees I wid-ened openings and explored, discovering her eventually. She had expired. Despite the humorous spectacle of my awkward and frantic chase and all the human scent

I had scattered about the area, I was elated to have taken a wood duck with my bow!

In order for a reader to better imagine the scenes, it is perhaps best to explain our pastures. These areas were either lumbered years ago or never forested and have native vegetation upon which cattle graze. Sometimes they are burned or chopped at intervals of many years and sometimes not, so how open or choked they are varies, but they cannot be thought of as short, flat, cleared land like a farmed field. The most overgrown ones can be twice as high as a man's head with myrtles, palmettos, maples and briars and present a challenge to penetrate.

A night or two past the full moon, having eaten and cleaned up, I stepped out of my trailer and noted the moon had risen and was spilling bright, silvery light on the deserted camp and pastures. There was an exceedingly open pasture west of our camp with a few thin, scraggly heads in it, but without sufficient cover to allow deer to move freely there in the daytime during rifle season. Nonetheless, I had hung a stand in a tiny head a while back planning an early morning or late afternoon sit sometime. The season was nearly over now and it was not likely I would get a chance to hunt there so, with my hard shadow leading the way and armed only with a video camera, I set out for the stand hopeful of witnessing nocturnal deer action which so far in my life I had done only on fleeting occasions in my headlights or, years ago, in spotlights when we used to perform deer counts for the ranch and with friends employed by the game commission. Both of these methods were intrusive and the deer knew we were there.

Perhaps halfway to the stand, I noticed the wild hogs. There were a good number of them dotting the open pasture. Hogs are not considered game animals and, as mentioned previously, it is therefore legal to hunt them at night. Intrigued by the prospect of moonlight stalking and shooting, I retraced my steps to camp, traded my bow, Bane Too, for the videocamera and hotfooted it back to the pasture.

Hogs abounded, some scattered and some in groups. Dew had already settled on the grass so the pasture, bathed in moonlight, glistened and sparkled. The natural beauty was so perfect that it made me feel lucky to witness it; to be part of it. Three does grazed in the pasture, their slender forms and graceful movements in ideal harmony with the gentle, luminous and lovely expanse. The view seemed magical to me.

Later, when I was crawling among hogs, ready to loose an arrow, I saw a buck perhaps forty yards distant and was again transfixed by the beauty as the moonbeams gleamed off his antler tips; accentuated the whiteness of his underside, and painted his body a soft copper. Later still, as I approached the still form of the big hog I'd arrowed, white ears caught my attention. Two does were watching me, alert and poised for instant flight and again the perfection of the scene, the wildness and beauty of the creatures and the gentle caresses of the moonlight struck me intensely.

Nine years before, after an evening meal and inspired by Maurice Thompson and his accounts of roaming Florida's wildlands by moonlight, I decided to stroll about the pastures a bit. I took one of my longbows, Moon Sliver, in honor of Maurice. Here follows the entry I jotted in my journal:

"Moon Sliver was out and about under a moon that was anything but a sliver. It was big, round, and bright and cast hard shadows where its light fell on shrubs or cypress. I had studied the moon as it rose at sunset with my binoculars and marveled at how three dimensional it looked, a giant globe in the sky, pale and beautiful amidst equally pale, pastel clouds.

It was not pale now and by its light I could easily see two hundred yards or maybe more. In fact cypress heads and myrtle stands over a thousand yards away stood out distinctly. The pasture sort of gleamed and the moonlight imparted a sense of beauty and mystery. I could picture how wondrous moonlight must render the snow-covered landscapes up north with everything glowing and still, crystal and quiet!

Before I walked too far, I could see the black shapes of hogs dotting the pasture as they rooted here and there. Quietly, I made my way toward two of the closest and could soon hear them ripping the grassy roots and throwing forward the sandy earth. One turned toward me. I kneeled and he approached, pausing to nose about as he came. As he passed broadside to me I could see he was a boar and slipped an arrow onto Moon Sliver's string and pulled back with the bow canted nearly horizontally. The arrow leapt from the bow soundlessly and then came the solid thwack of a good hit, but even the bright moonlight did not allow me to see where the dark arrow hit the black beast.

The hog raced north across the pasture and I feared he would head into a dark and shadowed cypress swamp so I ran after him, keeping toward the swamp side to encourage him eastward. His black companion looked up and fled as we pounded by on each side of him and my foot almost came down on a very large brown boar I had failed to see in some high grass. I actually had to lunge sideways to avoid kicking him and felt lucky to miss for his tusks might well have ripped my leg out of sheer reflex reaction. He went left and I to the right and then my hog entered some short, shadowy bushes and disappeared.

I had taken my eyes off of him during my near collision with the brown boar and was, at this point, unsure how far separated we had become. I scanned the pasture trying to glimpse his running form when suddenly I heard a wheezing, gasping breath followed by a slow, soft exhalation. He lay in some high grass in the shadow of a myrtle fifteen yards from where I had stopped, but, if not for the sound of his final breath, he would have been terribly difficult to discover.

I needed my truck to haul him out so I walked back toward camp with my mind enjoying the excitement and exhilaration of the stalk and chase. More hogs were visible to the east and the air felt pure and fresh. I paused and soaked in the dreamy and pretty spirit of the wilds by moonlight."

One November day, when giant wind formed seas eroded the beaches near my home mercilessly, I sat in Tyson creek at a place where a few tiny freshets joined the deeper main creek. With gusts over forty miles per hour, the wind brought me the sweet, earthy scent of the early morning swamp and stripped leaves from whipping tree limbs. Near me, a giant tree creaked and groaned for several seconds and then toppled loudly down as if in slow motion splintering lesser trees as it fell and punctuating its crash with a huge, white splash. Spotting an animal's movement could be quite difficult because the woods itself was a sea of motion. Ferns whipped, swayed, and thrashed. Shrubs and low branches arched and bowed and the trees rocked. The tree that held my stand, a fairly sturdy one, was no exception and I rocked and swayed along with the forest.

The approach of game would be hard to hear as well with all the sounds of leaves, limbs, and branch tips breaking and falling and tumbling about, but I did pick out the plash, plash, plash of something walking through water and from behind a small cabbage palm strode a good hog, jet black in color. It was obviously a boar hog and his lips were distended on each side of his snout from his curved canine teeth. Craig had asked me to get a hog for him if I got a chance and my dad had told me my uncle, Nick, would like one so, when the boar was four or five yards off, I drew Simplicity and felt the broadhead near my finger. I released and, with but a hushed whisper, the bow poured its energy into the arrow's launch. The boar stiffened and then let out an angry squeal as he ran a short half circle, falling dead eight yards from my tree.

Soon movement among all the other movement caught my eye and coming down a little slough was an alligator of eight feet. He was an incredibly able stalker, moving slowly and noiselessly and remaining motionless for long periods. Several branches and logs crossed the freshet and these he crossed by slipping over or under them without noise or abrupt motion. He flowed more then he crawled.

The hog was laying within three feet of the slough and the wind would carry his odor over the 'gator's path undoubtedly and I was apprehensive that I might need to climb down and protect my kill, but the 'gator gave no sign of smelling it and the big boar was hidden from sight by the surrounding knee-high ferns. Arriving at the deeper creek, the 'gator submerged except for the top of his head and remained motionless for at least a half an hour. Then I looked one time and he was gone.

A raccoon came down the same slough later yet. He was not alarmed so I assumed the 'gator left little scent or that the raccoon was regularly exposed to the scent. When the 'coon got abreast of the fallen hog however, he stiffened and stood erect. Some raccoons once had repeatedly attempted to steal one of my arrowed turkeys, but there was no need for alarm this time as the raccoon desired no part of what he was smelling and scooted quickly away.

This is the hog the 'gator passed. Note the ferns behind it that sheltered the hog from view.

I was once in a treestand watching the approach of six deer from the east. They were all antlerless, the smallest one probably six months old and it was distinguishable by color as well as size because it was a piebald. Its left side was primarily brown with only a few splotches of white, but it's right side was almost entirely white, speckled here and there with tan. As they drew even with me, an eight point buck raced out of some pines northwest of my tree and chased the little piebald with his antlers menacing and hooking. The small deer dodged the first rush and there is no telling what would have happened next because a poorly aimed arrow from my bow whizzed by the buck and all the deer fled. The buck came from upwind and, although I have witnessed bucks playfully chase younger deer, his attack seemed unquestionably earnest. He singled out the smallest deer, but it was also the most peculiarly colored and, in retrospect, I've wondered if the piebald was possibly a button buck.

My easiest drag of a hog is an entertaining story. Perhaps I shouldn't say easiest drag for, happily, hogs have tumbled in pastures where I could drive directly to them, but this time I was hunting far into the depths of the Bull Creek swamp, nearly to the other side. 'Deep Crossing' provided a route through and across the swamp yet only in times of prolonged drought could it be forded by an ordinary four-wheel drive truck like mine and on the day of this hunt if the water level differed from normal, it was on the high side. Anyhow, I guess 'easiest hog to clean' is the best description.

Some sows had rooted and milled about the area of my stand for some time when two big boars joined them with alacrity, burbling out peculiar grunts that sounded like the deep chortling of an exhaust pipe bubbling under water. I arrowed one of them and his death run took him even closer to the far edge of the swamp bottom. Billy had planned to hunt the woods beyond the creek and not long after I climbed into my stand before dawn that morning came the sound of his big swamp buggy crawling to the northwest. The buggy was loud enough that it could not have returned unnoticed in the still air so I pulled the boar to the track that parallels the creek bottom and stuck one of my brightly fletched arrows above it to attract his attention.

Moving my stand further back toward the center of the swamp, I hunted until afternoon. The wind picked up so I wasn't sure, but hints of sounds seemed to indicate the buggy had paused north of my new stand site and knowing Billy to always be helpful, I assumed the hog was picked up and heading back to camp.

Later when I reached camp the hog was nowhere to be seen. Billy was gone, but that was expected for he had told us he needed to leave early to participate in a charity golf tournament. Craig was nearby, shaking his head, and I strolled his way to question him, but before I could he asked me, "Can you believe that Billy? Talk about irresponsible! He comes into camp and drops a hog off at the cleaning station. Then he goes and showers, changes into his street clothes and leaves!"

"Yeah, where is the hog?"

Craig, still shaking his head answered, "I knew he wasn't coming back out this weekend so I cleaned it for him. How irresponsible can you get?"

I laughed a bit before I thanked him and explained why 'Irresponsible' Billy had just dropped the hog off and left.

The subject of cleaning hogs brings to mind another interesting occurrence. A friend from up north was down and quite keen to try for a hog with his recurve. Hunting together, we were fortunate to slip up on a group of good sized hogs and each simultaneously arrowed one. They both scaled in the 130's and taking the opportunity to verify the ratio between whole weight and dress weight on hogs, I weighed the gutted carcasses and both were in the 80's so the gut bucket held somewhere near one hundred pounds. My friend's broadhead had pulled free of his shaft and, not locating it in the muscle or hide, we concluded it must be in somewhere in the depths of the garbage can of innards. When we dumped the bucket's contents in the pasture, I marked the spot with an arrow thrust into the ground and we rushed back to camp to shower and change for an evening hunt. "The buzzards will have eaten everything by when we return at sundown," I assured him and for emphasis I steered toward the gut pile as we headed out to hunt thirty or forty minutes later, eager to let him see how quickly the scavenging birds descend on the bone-yard. Instead of the mass of big, black birds squabbling and jumping about that I expected, the pasture was barren.

"That's odd," I said. Not even one bird could be seen and usually red-shouldered hawks, eagles, and caracaras team up with the vultures. I was perplexed and felt a little discredited by their absence until we pulled closer and, below the marking arrow, found only a brown stain on the pasture's grass. In the middle of the stain lay one thing, my friend's arrowhead. People talk about eating like a bird, but whoever coined it probably hadn't witnessed birds consume nearly one hundred pounds of offal in less than forty minutes.

One afternoon I sat until dark with a couple spears in a stand. Several deer had come nearby, but the only one close enough for a spear throw was a six point, too small for our club antler requirements, so I merely videoed and watched and later, under the cover of darkness, moved the stand and cut some interfering branches and shrubs. By the time I had everything the way I wanted and started walking out toward the truck it was quite dark. If there was to be a moon that evening, it had not risen yet and as I left the woods and entered an overgrown pasture it grew no lighter. As usual I found my way along without a flashlight, but it was difficult.

As I describe what happened and my attending thoughts, this incident will seem drawn out, but I implore the reader to realize this all occurred in scant seconds.

A clump of palmettos not a yard ahead of me rattled and shook loudly and wildly and I assumed I had inadvertently startled and spooked something large like a big hog or a cow, but instead of the noise retreating, the palmetto shook more viciously and noisily and even against the dark sky I could see the taller fronds whipping about with a diabolically frenzied motion. The noise was not retreating, but advancing toward me and now I could see a big, black head level with my chest bearing down on me. I thought to yell to scare it off, but I intended just a single yell and I have no idea why the yell continued on and on. I thrust my spear below the head to stop the beast, but my spear hit nothing and the head was nearly on me. Still yelling, I jerked the spear up and bumped a turkey that flew within inches of my head. I'm sure I gave it a fright, but, believe me, no worse that it gave me!

I have never seen turkeys roost on the ground although I imagine they do when nesting. This was certainly not nesting season and I have no idea what this turkey was doing, but obviously the palmettos, briars, and vines entangled it and its frantic struggles to free itself as I approached so closely created the unbelievable commotion that alarmed me. What appeared to me as the head of a crazed, charging beast was actually the entire turkey. I assumed he flew toward me in an attempt to the reach the trees I had just left as there was only pasture in the other direction. Happily, none of my friends heard my yells so I wasn't called upon to explain them!

7

On the Trail

The raccoons were gone now and the woods seemed quieter and emptier without them though squirrels still leapt crashingly from palm frond to frond. Empty shells of oranges hung in the wild trees in the strand hardly discernable from the orange forms of the whole, uneaten fruit, but within a day or two they would dry and sag and look like dead, empty, brownish sacks. The raccoons, a big female with four nearly grown youngsters, had ascended the tree and edged out on narrow branches to push and claw at the ripe oranges near the stem attempting to penetrate the tough rind. If successful, the peel would give and the happy 'coon would cradle the orange and scoop out the sweet pulp. Some peels proved too resistant or the branch offered too little stability to allow the 'coon sufficient leverage and the abandoned fruit would be rendered pitted and scarred, but still whole. Occasionally, a stem gave way as a raccoon pushed and the orange thumped to forest floor. Later, when the 'coons climbed down from the trees they sniffed these out and had no trouble opening and eating them on the ground. I hoped they would inadvertently leave one or two whole and uneaten under the tree as raccoons often did, but on this afternoon, they found all that had fallen.

Motion east of me manifested the silent and timid movement of a doe. She stepped out of the ferns and small cabbage palms of the creek bottom from amid the trunks of water oaks, water elms, and palms. In front of the deer was a raised, sandy island in the swamp thick with saw palmettos and giant, rough live oaks. At this interface grew five sweet orange trees, three near my stand, one near the doe and one halfway between. She nosed around under the tree and finding no oranges, headed my way.

At the second tree she again found no whole oranges, but found the hollow rind of one the raccoons had eaten and either they had left a little of the fruit's flesh in it or a bit of the juice for she repeatedly put her nose into it and tried to lick its interior. She played with it for nearly ten minutes and several times it became stuck on her nose. Then when she would lift her head to scan for danger she looked like a cartoon character or a bizarre Rudolf with a large, perfectly round and bright orange nose!

Eventually, she abandoned the rind and walked to the trees a few yards from my stand. 'Deer Bane's' string sang its fast and quiet song and she raced northward. My stand was in the creek bottom at the southwest edge of the raised island and beyond the island was a cypress pond shrouded by thick myrtles and then some pasture. My ears recorded that she had continued north through the pond even though she was lost to sight within two or three bounds.

With good hits, I've never spooked a deer further by following up immediately and sure of such a hit now I took up the trail. It was fortunate I did because I can't imagine finding this deer if I hadn't. The blood sign was good and easy to follow, but in the pond, of course, became difficult and I had to search for blood or water splashed on the few leaves protruding from the water here and there. My progress was therefore slow and while I was so engaged, I heard some splooshing and looked up to see a doe at the myrtle edge of the swamp walk in a circle and then head toward me. I readied an arrow, but, unsure if it was my doe or another one, was hesitant to shoot. After approaching within 30 yards of me she turned broadside and walked to the east into the deepest portion of the pond. The water was well above her belly and there were no leaves there to record her trail. My boots full of water and wet to my waist, I followed as noiselessly as possible. The deer's head was low and its posture had none of the alertness that is so readily associated with whitetails, leaving me fairly certain it was the doe I shot. Sure enough, after seventy or so yards of eastward walking she laid her head gently between two trees and her body slid into the water. I waded up and her eyes were lifeless.

I resumed the blood trail to determine what had occurred. Once shot, she had dashed rapidly due north to the edge of the pasture. There she stopped and stood and then walked the circle I witnessed and back into the pond. Had I only the blood trail to go by, there would have been no evidence of her retracing her course and then branching off to the east. Her head wedged between two tree trunks would have been nearly impossible to spot without being right on top of it.

A bowhunting friend once told me that bowhunting was difficult and he divided the difficulty into equal thirds; the scouting and set up to get an opportunity at game being the first third, making the shot when the chance comes being the second, and finding the game after the shot being the final third. I've kept this notion in mind over the years and while on any one hunt one of his portions may not be equally difficult, in the long run all three are important. This chapter includes a few hunts that are notable primarily because of the challenge of the final third.

A thin strand of creek bottom woods between two overgrown pastures held a great deal of deer sign. The strand was thick with trees, understory, and vines, but over the past two years I had whittled out, with machete' and handsaw, a more open area at a natural crossing. Seeing that game was using it extensively, I placed a stand and one early morning climbed up into it. To reduce my scent trail, I had entered the strand further east and waded the flowing creek to the tree. The morning was one of those when time flies because the animals are so active. A big gobbler ghosted in out of the lush tangle of growth eastward when the light was still faint and the mists thick, early enough one would have expected turkeys to still be on the roost. My hiding place, despite the leafy branches above and below the stand, was not deceptive enough to fool his eyes and he scooted quickly and noiselessly away. The ground was moist with dew and dew drops from the leaves above struck earth and water and other leaves with mild 'plops' and 'plinks' and 'splisses'. When squirrels bounced about, around, and between limbs, showers of dew rained down loudly.

A deer in the thick pasture to the north offered several tantalizing glimpses, but its head was never visible and its roundabout course that seemed to be bringing it nearer turned out to be just a tease.

Moments later, plashing steps foretold of the approach of three deer. The first to emerge from the understory was a big doe. She paused about a yard from the base of my tree. 'Bane Too' was ready and my arrow leapt from its string and plunged through her chest. She wheeled back the way she had come, the two unseen deer splashing off with her, but then it sounded as though she turned north and they continued west. Several splashes from outside the swamp gave evidence she had fallen, probably 20-25 seconds after the shot.

I sat. A spike fed through the area for several minutes, at times no more that three or four yards away. Three black sows later did the same. Between myrtles outside the swamp, came a glimpse of a big bodied buck.

Game was definitely moving well and Florida laws allow two deer per day, but as mid-morning arrived, so did concerns that the doe may have not fallen in the shade. Binocular aided inspection revealed a blood trail starting right below my stand. Getting an exit wound from a nearly straight down shot is paramount for a decent blood trail and later I discovered the arrow had actually driven through her sternum (after slicing the aorta in route). Such penetration can largely be attributed to the very heavy shafts in concert with a 235 grain broadhead that I use.

Through the creek, its attendant fringe of tangled brush and briars, and a small aisle of pasture, the blood trail was readable and ended in a marshy pond amid even more brush and briars from where the final splashing sounds must of emanated. Try as I might I could not pick the trail up again from five yards into that pond. Investigating every possible continuation of her course exhausted more than an hour and left my spirits discouraged and perplexed. Perhaps the fourteenth or seventeenth time I revisited the last sure sign, I noticed the blood was strewn on both sides of the leaves.

She had entered and exited the pond at the same spot on the same trail and then somehow thrown herself into an incredibly thick tangle of grapevine and briars fifteen feet from the pond's edge. Extricating her proved difficult and time consuming as the vines were tenacious and interwoven and I had carried no machete'.

Surprisingly often, at the mystifying end of a good blood trail, I've discovered that the deer looped around or jumped backwards or somehow flopped in an unexpected direction.

Blood trails are interesting and can be surprising. One year, my friend Ozzie and I were lucky enough to be drawn to hunt Tosahatchee which was as good of hunting on public land as one could find in our region of Florida. It was divided into zones and we picked different zones the first day, but when he wounded a small buck that evening, we both picked his zone the next morning to search for it. The day was hot with the temperature passing 95° before noon. Despite our best trailing effort which lasted the entire morning and led us over 400 yards, we failed to find him although we heard something get up and run in front of us once.

I found a small grove of young live oaks that slanted upward through a wide smattering of saw palmettos. Long, nearly black acorns were falling. I set a stand, returned to the truck for a late lunch and rinsed off with a few gallons of water. It was mid-afternoon so I returned directly to the stand while Ozzie elected to wait until 5:00pm hoping it would begin to cool down.

Just up in my stand, drenched and dripping, I tried to wipe the sweat from my glasses, but had to replace them as I heard an animal moving. The deer, a spike buck stepped under me. Deer Bane was already drawn. A long scar, probably from a barbed wire fence, ran down his back. The arrow drove through his chest. He raced off, continuing in the direction he was heading and I could immediately see the bright red trail. I scurried down from my perch excitedly. Following the trail only a short ways, I looked ahead and saw the downed deer. There he was! How had the flies found him so quickly? They swarmed over him. I thought he was a spike, not a three-point. The realization hit me. This was Ozzie's deer! My spike was laying twenty yards farther along the trail. By the way, for this limited hunt, the state had requested hunters not to field dress deer so a biologist could do so, making observations and taking parasite samples. When we dropped off our two deer to be gutted, the biologist wasn't smiling and I didn't think my fresh spike was the reason!

A distinct and short blood trail on a deer that hurtled off with desperation carrying the arrow which had angularly transfixed it as it quartered away caused me great puzzlement. There was no hardship reading the conspicuous trail and the deer had fallen in less than sixty yards. My arrow was not in her or under her, nor had I seen it on the path she had fled. Searching for it, I retraced the route thrice more with no luck, but then noted it stuck in a tree trunk three feet or more above ground level. Apparently when she rocketed past, the protruding portion of the arrow drove into the trunk, the head imbedding into the bark and wood and then the shaft pulled free of the doe as she surged on forward. With my intent and focused eyes raking the ground for the blooded shaft, the elevated arrow had repeatedly escaped detection.

One Christmas Eve morning, I hunted a portion of the Bull Creek swamp bottom. Before relating the particulars of this hunt, I should confess that a week and a half before I shot a doe directly below my stand. The arrow drove into her chest, but failed to make an exit wound. With the abundance of trees and shrubs in the fertile swamp bottom, visibility was extremely limited and within fifteen yards the fleeing deer was lost to sight. I took a compass reading on the last sounds of her flight, but, nonetheless, failed to find her or any blood despite looking for hours and hours and hours. A couple days later, the buzzards gave away the spot she had fallen and I was even more dismayed to discover that I had searched within five yards of her at least twice without spotting her. She had only managed to make it eighty yards.

Terribly disturbed by losing the deer and by the lack of penetration that resulted in the absent blood trail, I made three changes. I switched bows from the longbow to my Schafer recurve "Whispering Magic". (I still believe wholeheartedly in longbows, having taken much and quite large game with them, but having lost an animal made me want to take no chance of it happening again.) I changed broadheads. Lastly, I convinced myself to shoot longer distances if possible instead of always waiting for point-blank range. Because of the angle, at 15 or 20 yards the arrow does not need to drive in as deeply to provide an exit wound as it would at two yards. Exit wounds for me have always been paramount to provide the best blood trail. (In the years since this hunt, I actually went back to Black Widow recurves, heavier shafts and heavy broadheads. Now, I've resumed using a longbow, but have stuck with the heavy shafts and heads.)

Back to Christmas Eve morning in the swamp not far from the site the doe had fallen…her carcass now reduced to nearly nothing by the attention of coyotes, buzzards, and probably hogs. Forty yards north of me, through trunks and branches, flickering movement revealed thin legs and brown patches several times throughout the first few hours of light as deer came near me. Despite the sign in the vicinity of my stand, the deer seemed to favor the swamp just north of me, but eventually a doe fed toward me. I passed on some close shots waiting for a more distant quartering away shot. The opportunity didn't come until she was leaving and I had to shoot between two trees. I rushed the release and missed badly and completely.

About 10:30, I moved my stand to where I had seen deer earlier. A big, reddish raccoon and some wood ducks made my wait enjoyable and a little before noon two does sniffed for acorns a few yards from where my stand had earlier been. Within 25 minutes however, they had neared my new tree. One doe was huge and I took a twenty yard, slightly quartering away shot. Whispering Magic whispered and the arrow skewered her neatly.

Both does raced to the west, but as the stricken doe disappeared beneath the fronds she veered northwest and splashed tremendously through a creek. North of my tree, four such channels basically paralleled one another and, not surprisingly, I heard three more great splashes; all close, all within forty-five yards. Faced with lugging her out, cleaning her and still getting home in the early afternoon for Christmas Eve, I immediately climbed down and took up the trail. Walking the way she ran, I crossed the first creek at a spot shallow enough for the water not to go over my boots and found big splashes of water and blood on the two yard wide strip of ground that rose between the first two creek channels. Skirting back to a place shallow enough to cross the second creek, I came back up to another narrow rise of land expecting to find more of the fresh and obvious trail, but could not. Every possible route gave me no sign. If she had turned and ran in the creek west she would have to come out somewhere, but its banks displayed no evidence of her passing. If she doubled back down the creek to the east she would have passed within twelve yards of my stand. The splashing sounds of her flight gave evidence she had run west and then northwest.

An hour had gone by. Many of the possible pathways funneled to the remains of my unrecovered deer and redoubled my resolve to find this one. Walking north to the edge of the hardwood swamp, I searched east and west. Surely she would have to leave a trail through the thick palmettos that make the nearly impenetrable fringe, but repeatedly I found nothing. Two hours had elapsed and I was no closer than after the first four minutes. Incredibly frustrated, I realized I would probably be late for Christmas Eve with my entire family. The blood trail had started so strong and easy and now I was casting about with no evidence and with small hope. How, with a good shot and a decent trail could my search be so fruitless?

The answer provided itself by luck. As I extended my search along the swamp edge further and further, I eventually ended up well east of my stand although I didn't realize it at the time or I would not have come so far. My ears had proof that she did not head east of a line northwest of the stand and they would have heard her splash through the water or crash through the palmettos if she had doubled back. Anyhow, attempting to head south from the swamp edge, find my stand, and start over again for perhaps the eleventh time to discover where I went wrong, I encountered a deep part of a creek. Surveying for a spot to ford it, I spotted a small patch of brown near the opposite bank. It could be a submerged log or sinking debris, but it could be a deer below the surface. That proved to be the case.

She had died in the second creek and the extra splashes I heard must have been her death throes and the current had silently taken her back east of my stand while I was climbing down and trailing her. If an underwater branch hadn't caught her she may have been hundreds of yards away for the four creeks combine to make one deep one just a little further downstream. The area with four streams have deeper places, but there are so many shallows and blockages that I had never seen or heard of a deer actually drifting away.

Fishing her from the deep, swift waters was troublesome and the tote out memorable because a hurricane earlier in the fall had broken down so many trees in the swamp, but I made it to our Christmas Eve gathering on time and felt wonderfully happy to find this deer.

Blood trails that start well and end abruptly are particularly puzzling. One November we had several days of all time record breaking heat with temperatures in the nineties, no wind and mosquitoes that remained active the entire day and on the dark, fog choked morning of one such day, I climbed a tree deep in the swamp. Hogs had been squealing and grunting during my approach and climb and now suddenly a huge ruckus broke out quite close. Bow in hand, I tried to discern them through the fog and amid all the low cabbage palms. Something moved to left of all the fierce grunts and I assumed it was another hog, but discovered it was a buck with its neck stretched out and its legs braced, repeatedly lowering its head while still keeping its nose forward. The drooping fronds must have impeded his view of the noise-some boars and he bobbed his head in an attempt to better his vantage.

He was twenty yards and broadside and a tempting target, but I needed to be sure he would meet our club's antler requirements. My binoculars helped in the low light under the nearly solid canopy of the swamp and revealed him to be a decent eight point, but by then he'd had enough of the hogs and tip-toed back to the east, enveloped immediately by the low cabbage palms. He was again briefly in the clear at thirty-five yards, but walking and I hadn't enough confidence to risk the shot.

The air moved little and the misty vapors hung motionless. Here and there slices of light manifested its thickness. The leaves and fronds sweated and dripped. A doe fed along at times within ten yards. Mosquitoes hoarded around; dancing, whining, lightly touching and landing, relentless and persistent in their quest for my blood.

A buck stepped out no more than ten yards off, the young cabbage palms having sheltered his approach. After videoing him for a minute, I readied Bane Too. By now he was nearly below me and head first toward my tree. Fearing his response should he catch my scent at the base of the tree, I felt it would not be prudent to wait for a quartering away shot. Things happened fast; the light 'thunk' of the bow, the 'ssshep' of the arrow whisking through the buck, the great spurt of blood erupting from his back! He crashed off.

I picked out a landmark for his course and another for the last place I heard him. The big spurt of blood indicated an aortal hit. I scanned the ground with my binoculars and could see no blood and this made me question whether perhaps the spurt was only a figment.

A spike fed about and I videoed him. When he was within a few yards of the blooded arrow, he became uneasy, nosing several of the green ferns and walking away. I viewed the arrow again with binoculars and I couldn't believe it! Perhaps the light was different now, but the blood trail started right at the arrow and continued unbroken for the eight yards before it disappeared beneath the palm fronds, brightly splashing everything with red, bubbly blood. Elated, I climbed down. In all my years of bowhunting, I had never seen a trail start so thickly so quickly. I followed happily and unworriedly with the treestand on my back since he ran toward one edge of the swamp and I was deep enough in not to want to retrace my steps. It would be easier to drive the truck around to a different pasture then to drag a big buck over and around cypress knees and fallen trees and through the mud for an extra five or six hundred yards.

The trail stopped abruptly with a giant splash against a palm frond twenty yards from my tree. How could such a tremendous blood trail disappear? Circling about, I experimented with possible routes for fifteen minutes or so. Then, depressed, I returned to the start, unshouldered the stand, and dug in for some meticulous tracking, thinking of my friend Mack who had access to a great bloodhound and also had a young beagle himself, but who also happened to be in the Cayman Islands at the time.

To shorten a long story, occasional pinpoints of blood ten to fifteen yards apart, a bent fern, a loose piece of soil on a leaf stretched the trail to seventy yards over an hour and a quarter period; and the first twenty yards were blatant. In the regular fashion of following each probable travel course for twenty or so yards searching for any evidence to confirm or refute it as his flight path, I stumbled upon him. He had fallen mid leap and died upright, his front legs stretched forward and his rear ones bent below him as if ready to spring. He was beautiful.

The broadhead had severed the aorta and he hadn't made it eighty yards. The exit wound opened his belly and a wad of intestines the size of a large fist pushed through it sealing the hole unbelievably well. He weighed 152 pounds live weight, but that was on a scale. Dragging him through the swamp, tree stand on my back, bow in my hand, sweat drenching my clothes and running down my face, I may have allocated him a different weight.

I'm not sure there are any secret techniques to blood trailing. Obviously, it requires persistence and perseverance; looking for the tiniest traces of evidence of the animal's course, investigating all possible avenues for proof of or against its passage, and remembering to consider an animal backtracking or leaping from the trail. Blood is a welcome sign and undeniable evidence and even sheds light on the nature of the wound, but the best trackers look for any sign that suggests an animal's path. These indications may be as subtle as a broken spider web or disturbed dew, leaves turned differently from others, and faint edges impressed on leaves or other terrain that resists recording tracks. Sign is often at knee height or higher rather than on the ground. Mortally struck game oftentimes scuds away with abandon and leaves broken twigs or branches, tugged vines, or bent stems in its wake. One habit I've developed that is quite helpful is to always ascertain three bits of information immediately after the shot whether hunting from the ground or a stand. First, it is worth picking an exact reference as to where the animal was when hit. Next, I use my compass to determine the precise position where it disappeared from view and lastly, again with the compass I take a bearing on the last sound of its retreat. At different times each of these precautions has proved immensely worthwhile.

Over the years, I have, at the end of a blood trail, discovered that another predator had found the stricken animal before me. Coyotes are quite adept and notorious for this tendency and can consume a great deal of the carcass in an amazingly short time. In my experiences with them, they generally start at the rear end and take gouging bites from the hams. Their reputation causes one to think twice about leaving a wounded deer overnight, but this is not the only time to consider coyotes. I arrowed a deer an hour and a half after sunrise and remained on the stand until mid-morning. The blood trail led to a disappointing surprise. The doe was ravaged so completely that no meat was salvageable. A friend slew a deer in the afternoon, maybe 4:00 and dragged it to a place he could drive. Despite the human scent on and around the deer, in the short while required for the walk to his truck and the drive back, coyotes had eaten chunks out of the hind quarters. He had caught no glimpse of the perpetrators and was quite astonished upon returning to his kill. Although in our area their scat occasionally contains hog hair, I have never arrowed a hog and found it molested by coyotes. Of interest and perhaps shedding some light on this, some of the dogs I've seen trail wounded game are rewarded with a small piece of meat from the found carcass and appear to relish deer or turkey, but disregard any offering of hog.

Bobcats, too seem to favor deer and after feeding typically attempt to cover the carcass with leaves and dirt and most often drag it a ways despite the animal's weight being at least three and sometimes more than four times their own weight. Twice I've witnessed exceptions to this when the game was neither dragged nor covered, but both times the bobcat was resting within ten yards of the food source. Interestingly, both of the animals were hogs and both had been eviscerated by the cat. On one of them, even though the hog was disemboweled, it appeared the bobcat had fed only on the cheek and neck.

In north Florida, I hunted from a stand hung in an incredibly dense thicket. After a hit I feared [wrongly] might be a gut shot and with low temperatures forecast for the evening, I waited until the following morning to pursue a doe. A bloody area showed where she had fallen within fifty yards of my stand, but then a drag trail began evidenced by crushed and broken plants and tufts of fur. She had been dragged over stumps and fallen logs that were difficult to straddle. A bear had found her. Her hams were undamaged, but a backstrap had been eaten and access to her peritoneal cavity achieved at the kidney region. A shoulder had been ripped, not bitten, off and it was missing and not to be found. Imagining the strength to tear off the shoulder ripping skin and all was mind staggering. We were able to secure and utilize the hindquarters and one shoulder.

8

Some Stalks on Deer

Treestand hunting has an undeniable appeal; the careful scouting, the plotting of the ambush, the wait on the stand with hopes high watching nature unfold its secrets, anxiously scanning for evidence that the plan will succeed or for information on how to improve it. All aspects of such a hunt make it an enjoyable challenge!

Like icing on the cake, the treestand hunter gets to witness beautiful scenes and memorable occurrences. At the same time, who can deny the irresistible allure of stalking deer? The excitement of taking the hunt to the game? The application of keen observation and woodsmanship? I can't help but to embrace both methods so let me here record a few stalks.

One afternoon while slipping through an oak scrub, I spied two does striding into a little cove shaped by a half circle of oaks. As soon as they progressed far enough to be unable to see me, I ran to the cove silently in the white, sugary sand and then eased from palmetto clump to clump closing the distance to less than fifteen yards. Not wanting to arrow the young one, I waited until they separated. The larger one started to head toward me and disappeared behind the thin strip of palmettos I was using for cover. The smaller one followed. A deer's back then showed over a low spot in the palmettos two yards from me and I drew ready to drive an arrow from unbelievably close range. At that second however, I noticed a deer in the location from which they had come and it was a full sized mature doe. I let down the little longbow 'Daddy' now convinced the chest I was aiming at was the youngster. The close deer then stepped through the palmettos and her head, no more than a yard away, was long and mature. Snorting, she wheeled off with a whitetail's remarkable agility and speed and her fawn, a couple of yards behind her followed suit. Needless to say, the other doe whose presence confused me enough to cost me a point blank shot, was gone as well. My bow and I were alone in an empty area of woods.

Still hunting late one morning, I descried a deer and crept closer. Discovering it was a large racked buck accompanying a long-headed doe, I stalked with great care to within twenty-eight yards and kneeled hidden behind a palmetto clump, the last bit of cover. The bearing of each deer was relaxed and unsuspicious. Many unforeseen events can affect a hunt and, at this point, a turkey stepped around my very clump and, seeing me, exploded into loud, frantic flight. Both deer stared at my clump, heads up and bodies tense, poised for flight. Several minutes passed before they resumed feeding and even then, they remained wary and their heads were up most of the time. In fact, the buck only dropped his head to browse six times in the next twenty minutes.

I managed to capture their images on the video recorder, but then put it away and readied my longbow. They were so edgy and also an opportunity could present quickly and fleetingly. Without cover to advance, it seemed most prudent to wait for their move. A hen turkey fed past at six yards and disappeared into the palmettos to the south without sighting me.

Eventually, the doe walked to the northwest and stepped behind a leafy myrtle. The buck then moved from a bushy area to the more open place where she had been feeding and stood broadside at twenty-eight yards. I drew Daddy, but could not find the comfortable, confident, natural feeling that usually presages my good shots. Instead, it seemed my eye was trying to determine if the arrow was pointing where it should. In the prior year I had been deliberately practicing longer distances and surprised myself with the accuracy I could achieve, but on this shot it seemed too risky. In all likelihood, he would follow the doe and she was now in an area of scattered myrtles, ideal for stalking. The wind was holding steady and right. I eased up on the tight string and the longbow's limbs relaxed.

I was again awed by the massiveness of the buck's antlers as he turned and traced the doe's steps. As soon as he disappeared, I ran lightfootedly to the myrtle and peeked around it. The buck was there, six or seven yards away and oblivious to me. Unhappily, there was another turkey also, this one on my myrtle's far side and it flapped wildly and loudly as it took to the air. The deer were gone in an instant, snorts, thuds, and splashes giving testimony to how quickly and completely they were gone. Splashes in a pine copse seventy yards distant gave evidence of even more spooked deer.

Interestingly, everyone who watches the video is amazed at this buck's rack, but close inspection reveals a lack of brow tines, so despite his impressive proportions, he was a six point. It is really thought provoking how often an unusual buck is spotted and never seen by any of us again. Five years have passed since I videoed this one and no one has reported so much as a glimpse of him.

The water was high; higher than any of us had seen before and, with the wet year that preceded it, the ground was so saturated that all the rain water just sat there and made marshes of the pastures and lakes with ducks in places I had never seen standing water before. It was difficult to drive anywhere without becoming stuck.

The deer had lately been feeding in the open pasture on hairy indigo. This year it was so abundant that the deer didn't need to move and could eat for hours and the indigo was so widespread that the deer could feed anywhere. Predicting precisely where they would be or where they would pass was a guessing game.

The water had brought out mosquitoes in vast numbers and the two main species in the pasturelands are very aggressive throughout the entire day. These are the large black ones and the huge 'gallon gulpers' that can bite through multiple layers of nearly any clothing. Both types share a common trait; they are not prone to buzz around one much, preferring to land quickly and bite immediately. This is in contrast to the mosquitoes of the swampwoods. There, the mid-sized brown ones land without a lot of fanfare and are thereby easily killed. Also, they restrict the height of their activity to the first and last few hours of the day. The other types found in the woodland habitat are smaller and so light that their touch-downs on one's skin are barely perceptible and they annoyingly buzz and brush and flit and hover around one in great numbers, taking forever to land and being skittish and relentless all at once. The tiniest variety actually has a sharp, stinging bite not at all in proportion to its size and pays no heed to time of day, happy to provide a minor vexation at any hour. Anyhow, the species involved in this account are the first mentioned aggressive ones.

One late afternoon, slipping through a pasture, I spotted a deer feeding next to a small strand of scrub. My binoculars revealed that she was a doe and apparently solitary. With the wind steadying from the northeast, I sneaked to the strand well south of her and employed its cover to close the distance. A fox trotted by a scant few yards ahead without noticing me. Some deer were in the pasture east of the scrub as well and I edged toward them since they were closer. At that point some turkeys ran off, spooked either by the fox or me. The fox stopped seven yards north of me, turned and sat watching me with a bored looking face. It was almost like he was looking at me and wondering how he could hunt with me blundering about behind him and scaring the game.

As I progressed toward the east deer, I quickly learned there were at least four in the group and I decided to leave them for the time being and resume my stalk on the original deer preferring the fewest eyes, ears, and noses.

With good fortune, I closed to within fifteen yards, but she was facing directly my way. Mosquitoes were biting through my clothes, but finally she moved behind a bit of oak brush that shielded me from her eyes. Brushing some of the mosquitoey horde away, I started scooting forward to be in position for an easy broadside shot, but a second deer chose that instant to step out six yards in front of me. Unsure about my crouched form, she stared and stared and stamped and stared and caused great happiness in the mosquito world as I dared not move. She wheeled away and blew a few more times from the pasture, out of sight, beyond the scrub. Assuming my original doe had fled as well, I started to move. The doe was still there, but lost no time vanishing when she saw me.

Having blown a good stalk twice left me discouraged. The stalk awaiting me on multiple deer and less cover would be more difficult. My approach involved crawling on my hands and knees or at times my belly, pushing my bow ahead and pulling some of the cactus spines out of my hands as I went and leaving some to remove later. Finally, ensconced in a patch of palmettos, I counted the deer and discovered fourteen does, none of which was more than forty-five yards distant and some as near as twenty. Over the next twenty minutes they all came closer and closer to me although they barely had to move to eat because of how thickly and prolifically the hairy indigo was growing.

The largest doe had been within easy range the whole time, but always at a head on angle. At ten yards she turned broadside and none of the other deer appeared to be looking my way. Bowhunters know the feeling of the hard, tight string against the fingertips, the tightening shoulder and back muscles that sense the power of the bending limbs, and the still, calm, deadly shaft anchored near the lip and stretching ahead. The arrow sped from Deer Bane and the stricken doe dropped.

The other deer flared out in all directions at the sound of the bow and her peculiar behavior, but then regrouped and kept looking at her with nervous curiosity; inching forward, bounding back, and coming forward again. One doe was ten yards from me and broadside so I drew Deer Bane and let another arrow fly. This doe was so nervous and tense that I should have known better. She spun about and maybe the arrow caught her in the flank, but it was all too fast for my mind to be sure. She ran off fifty yards or so and stood looking back.

Now more deer came up to investigate the downed doe including a big doe with silvery white sides, apparently a beautifully symmetrical piebald with a whitish sheen down the neck and both shoulders, narrowing toward the flank. Her whole coat was smooth and silvery. I would have attempted to arrow her and tanned the skin, but I thought there was a chance that I had taken two deer as my second deer was still standing not too distantly and two is our daily bag limit. The piebald and other does returned to the downed deer repeatedly sometimes passing as close as five yards from me over the next twenty-five minutes.

Daylight would soon begin to fade and I needed to pick a route for my truck to cross the soggy pasture without sinking to its axles and maybe trail a deer as well, so as much as I disliked spooking the deer, I stood and waved my arms. Deer bounded off in all directions including my second target. She ran without any indication of her wound across the east end of the pasture. I was still concerned that the arrow may have thrust forward into her innards and cast about for a trail or sign of the wound. A few long, white hairs were on the grass and indigo where she was struck and my arrow lay twenty yards or so beyond (not the direction she ran), a scant bit of blood on part of the broadhead, but the shaft was dry and clean. The arrow must have grazed her lightly.

I managed to get a photograph of the unique and beautiful piebald and her offspring the last day of deer season the following year. She was forty yards off, too distant for the picture to convey fully her graceful loveliness, but near enough to display the silvery white portions of her coat which were so distinctive. Two of my friends encountered her in the following years. Skip saw her twice distantly from treestands and dubbed her "Silversides". Five years after my stalk Don, another traditional bowhunter and not a superstitious person was hunting from a stand in the swampwood not too far from an ancient cowhunter shack. It had probably once been a hard claimed little island of a man's influence in the big wilderness that was the Florida interior, but now it was mostly collapsed and the lush forest had reclaimed it. In the gloaming light under the dense swamp canopy, Don was startled to see a faint, ghostly white apparition float about the vicinity of the shack's remnants. It hovered above the ground and silently moved here and there and at times stayed quite still. After a while, it approached nearer and he could make out the brown legs and body of the doe and he made a good twelve yard shot with his recurve to secure this unique deer. He had the hide tanned and it is incredibly striking. When I began writing this account, I talked with Don to be sure my memories of his hunt were accurate and after he finished recounting the details of his adventure he said that he was sure glad she came toward him.

"Yes, it is a beautiful hide." I said, agreeing on his good fortune.

"No", he responded, "I don't mean necessarily that I got the shot. If she had milled around and then ventured off some other direction from the shack I would still be convinced today I had seen a spirit."

This was a distinct and easily recognizable deer that inhabited our hunting grounds at least nine years, but, even with us hunting the land fairly hard from September through January and moderately from January through April (small game and turkey seasons), she was only seen five times. Like all deer, she was a bit of a spirit!

Against a northeast wind on an October morning, I slipped along a dike. On the east side was a low hedge of palmettos and beyond it was pasture of varying degrees of openness. The other side had pasture as well, but it was more choked with palmettos and along the ditch many shrubs and trees had grown to where there were few places to view much of that pasture. Quite early, I spotted a tremendous buck to the east, nose out and head down, half running across the pasture with that distinctive, stiff-legged gait of a trailing buck. He zigged and zagged a few times, but then disappeared quickly to the east.

Continuing along, disappointed the trail hadn't taken him toward me, I spotted another great buck, slightly smaller the first coming from the north, northeast. I was ready. Like the first buck when he hit the first part of the trail when it turned abruptly eastward, he milled around and I grunted with my mouth. He looked my way and I hoped he might believe the sound came from the doe he was trailing, but he put more credence in his nose and followed the other buck's path.

After traversing a couple hundred more yards, I caught sight of a third buck. This one's rack was smaller yet, but still quite respectable and while not massive, bestowed upon him a noble carriage. He too was northeast of me, but his route appeared to be taking him northwest so after picking a few landmarks for guidance, I crept through the ditch and ran north behind the screen of shrubs. Upon reaching my landmarks, with stealthy caution, I clambered up the dike and peered over a palmetto into the eastern pasture hopeful for a close opportunity. Alas, he had crossed ten yards ahead of me, but a myrtle obscured my view of him as I neared the spot and he looked back to see me rise onto the dike. With two high bounds his flashing tail vanished into the myrtles and palmettos.

Sometimes the range of emotions and speed with which they flash by when bowhunting is absolutely amazing. A bowman can experience awe, nervous anticipation, excitement, astonishment, anxiety, disappointment, hope, accomplishment, and respect for nature in any order at any time. I had been flooded with many feelings, but the morning still held two more experiences in store.

Not much further along the dike was a doe feeding quietly forty yards to the east. As I watched her, movement to the north shifted my attention to another deer that also appeared to be a doe heading south, but with the same posture as a trailing buck. The deer continued with a fast, dogged pace and neck extended so persistently that I raised my binoculars to verify my eyes and discovered the small spikish antlers. The buck drew even with the doe and looked at her, but resumed the scent trail. The doe's earlier path meandered and curved for thirty or so yards southward and then turned back north and led directly to her. With the scent trail confirmation, this time he did not ignore the doe, which had returned to feeding after his first pass. He deliberately approached her. She shied away and he unhesitatingly closed again. The doe ran northwest in quick bounds and crossed the dike fifty yards ahead of me with the spike in pursuit no more than twenty yards behind her. They were then lost to sight, but I recorded the whole episode on video since I had no inclination to be ready for a shot. It is informative to watch deer behavior on such a tape noting postures, eye contact, and the interest the deer display. This young buck's behavior gave me much food for thought. Many times when spying a buck scent trailing a doe, I have attempted to lure him from the trail with grunts, bleats, or antler rattling reasoning that he would believe the doe came my way and head over to save time and gain on the doe, but only very rarely had it been the least bit effective. In fact, earlier the same morning a buck ignored my grunts in favor of the invisible and apparently tantalizing trail. This spike had a doe in view and no more than ten yards distant, but rather than check her out directly, he preferred to stick with the trail. Obviously, it is not easy to distract a buck from such a trail.

Several hundred yards passed below my feet before I saw another deer. It was a buck, but the fleeting image between palmettos gave the impression it was young. The pasture on both sides of the dike was much more overgrown here, but a firebreak had been cut a few years before forty yards to the east and the buck seemed to be walking south along it. With the northeast wind still blowing, I crept through the brush and palmettos southeastward to cut him off using the utmost care to avoid making a sound. As I readied Simplicity, a Tommy Allen longbow, and watched the firebreak, a four-point came by on the far side of the hedge beyond the firebreak from the south. Stymied, I tried to puzzle out how the buck had gotten south of me without my awareness and why he had turned around. My mind was still confused and perplexed when another four-point, the original, came down the firebreak, leapt through the hedge and began sparring with the other. Again having no desire to arrow either of these small bucks, I quivered my arrow and unholstered the video camera. The two youngsters would push and shove, shake their heads and turn about, but then disengage simultaneously and look about as if by mutual or prearranged agreement. Then after an interval that varied in length each time they would relower their heads and resume the low keyed pushing match. I was within eight yards, but the hedge interfered greatly with the footage I was recording so I tried to slip through it and on one of their instantaneous and unexpected pauses one buck must have seen me and they bounded back, curious and looking, but eventually circling downwind and evacuating the area. Interestingly, they ran off in different directions.

It was a still hunting morning when I never launched an arrow or even drew back my bow, but it gave me as much enjoyment and excitement as any I can remember. I could ramble on for a long time about still hunting with its various blown opportunities and joyful successes, about a ten point buck with heavy, thick beams that swept hard forward parallel to his nose ridge and then upturned dramatically in their final few inches at twenty yards and does at less then a yard with the surprise in their eyes exceeded by the speed of their reflexes, about arrowing an alert but bedded deer, and about stalks on countless hogs. All in all, still-hunting offers an unbelievable amount of fun and excitement and education. Hopefully the few accounts I've chronicled will offer the reader the flavor of such endeavors.

9

Bows

It is surprising how quickly and enjoyably time passes with a bow in hand, wandering about, picking a tuft here or leaf there and sending a shaft toward it in a long, blurred streak. The feeling of the bow's handle in the archer's grasp, the quiet power of the limbs, the innocent arrow pointing vaguely ahead, and the freedom of the release in the moment preceding the susurrous flight all contribute to the enchantment of watching the arcing missile plunge to or near its target. The sum of all these feelings and perceptions and the interplay of mind, eye, and muscle yields a simple, magical quality that is bewitching and addicting. Who can be immune from its enjoyment?

When I would practice in my backyard, children of a wide assortment of ages would come over to watch and participate. Whenever I brought light bows and arrows to a gathering with youngsters they were in constant use and demand and I've had the same luck bringing bows, arrows and targets to get-togethers with adults. Add a moving target and people line up for turns. Undeniably, there is something attractive and wholeheartedly fascinating about the bow and arrow and the sport of archery.

I've been a lover of bows as long as I can remember, shaping crude ones from sticks and bamboo and various scrap materials until my first solid fiberglass bows. The very first was a Ben Pearson, followed by a Fred Bear model. It cracked and after I wrote the company, they sent me a new one. I was impressed at a very young age with the integrity of the company and purchased only Bear recurves for the next twenty years. I have several Bear bows in my collection and enjoy them all, especially my first wood and glass laminated bow purchased new around 1970. Back then, 55 pounds seemed stiff and powerful. I used it for turkey hunting this past season. It still shoots fast and is one of my quietest hunting recurves.

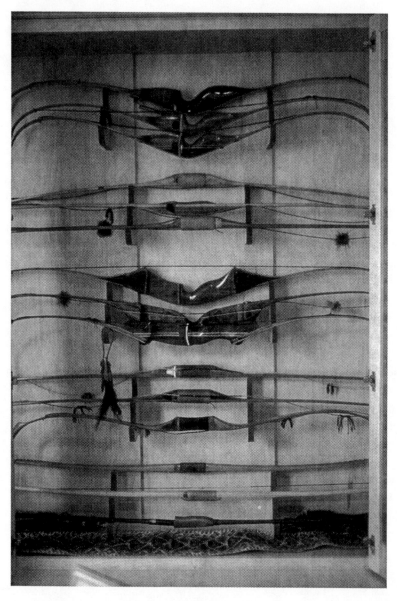

A few bows.

Over the years, I began collecting longbows and recurves driven by my passion for them as both tools of archery and works of art. Each bow has its own characteristics that affect its beauty and its functionality; the smoothness of its draw, the sweetness of its cast, the way it points and handles, the quiet music of its spring.

I've named the bows I use the most, partly out of romance and partly to simplify my record keeping as I write my journals since my collection contains multiple bows by certain bowyers differing sometimes only slightly or other times dramatically and a name is a much simpler denotation than a complete description. There is no space nor reason to list them all, but I will describe a few whose names have come up in these pages.

My first Black Widow, an MAII, I named Deer Bane and it has helped me harvest many, many whitetails, countless hogs, some elk and lots of other game. I've taken more whitetails with this one bow than any of my others primarily because I used it exclusively for so many years. That being the case, I have a special fondness for it. It is a wonderful bow and shoots perfectly predictably. The only things that lured me away from it were the quietness and simpleness of longbows. Deer Bane was fast, deadly accurate, but comparatively loud. I still have it and love to shoot it and even hunt with it at times. When I had difficulty with penetration with a long bow I had been shooting followed by a period of inconsistent accuracy, I returned to Deer Bane and the trouble was solved. The bow I use predominately now is merely a modern version of it. Black Widow crafts dependable, hard hitting, and accurate bows.

Moon Sliver, a Tommy Allen longbow was my first longbow that I used for hunting. It is quiet and a pleasure to draw and shoot, but light in draw weight. I've had good luck with it on deer and hogs, but worried always about the possible lack of penetration. A bow of osage orange and with nocks similar in shape to those fashioned formerly from cowhorn, it is appealing to the eye in color, shape and symmetry and looking at it as I write makes me yearn to fling some heavy arrows from its quiet string.

A Shafer recurve by Dave Windauer, named Whispering Magic took some hogs and deer as well, including a very special buck. Bent Medicine is a tiny Texas Recurve that is both remarkably fast and silent, even quieter than most longbows. Regretfully, it stacks badly and I could never develop a consistent feel for it and even though it took a couple deer and hogs for me, I carried it for only a season or two. I have a Black Widow longbow that again has been instrumental in several deer hunts and hog hunts that I call Frilless. It shoots impeccably, and its arrows penetrate the best of any of my longbows, but it does thump louder and sharper than most longbows.

Simplicity is a distinctive Tommy Allen longbow with a reverse handle design that renders its appearance awkward unstrung yet graceful and lovely braced.

Adding to its uniqueness, its limbs do not bend symmetrically and the upper limb exceeds the lower in length, vaguely suggestive of traditional Japanese bows. It is superbly smooth and pleasurable to shoot and has taken much game for me including my first longbow bull elk and many deer. It is a singular and special bow.

Breanna, my daughter, named my two Ron La Clair Shrew bows Daddy and Furry. They were maneuverable, easily strung and carried, fast and accurate and I enjoyed them thoroughly. In fact, I thought of them as the ultimate bows because of their ease of use and functionality and quietness. Unfortunately, I had difficult trails on a few deer and lost one because of a lack of an exit wound. Even though the bows had earlier taken many deer without trouble, I put them up (and sold one) after losing the doe (mentioned earlier in the text) and have used only recurves since. I may change my mind again someday and take 'Daddy' back to the woods because it is a lot of fun to shoot. (In fact, I have with good success since my first draft of this book.)

Bane Too is a Black Widow SAV and it shoots as precisely as Deer Bane, but it's faster, smoother and handles a wee bit better. With the heavy arrows it propels, its thump is dull and quiet and its penetration never lacking. Perhaps all the years with its namesake make shooting it natural for me, for the arrows I release from it often seem to find their mark with little conscious effort. It is phenomenally enjoyable to shoot in both field and woods.

Just recently, I was fortunate enough to acquire a Double Carbon Express longbow from Eddie Francisco and I am totally amazed by it. Arrows seem to magically zip from it to wherever I am focused no matter how small a target. Speed-wise it is incredible, yet it is a joy to shoot and as noiseless as a stalking tiger. I've never shot a sweeter bow and it is lovely in appearance as well. Eddie's craftsmanship and attention to detail stand out and render the bow special. Its name is Mellifluwood and since I haven't hunted with it yet, its moniker won't be encountered in the text, but my enthusiasm for it forbade any omission from a partial list of my bows.

I'm lucky enough to have many more bows, named and unnamed, but all unique and beautiful. Some are handmade, some antique, and some foreign (including one from Bhutan where the national sport is archery). The differences in them are considerable, but they share an innate beauty, a pleasing essence that must stem from each aspiring toward a common functionality, so even just looking at these graceful elements of archery holds a definite pleasurable charm.

10

Hunters, Whitetails, and Other Animals

Animals beside deer can become involved in deer hunts. True enough, the presence and behaviors of various species provide interesting entertainment to help keep one alert and excited and in tune with the woodland environment, but some become even more involved; actually influencing the outcome of the hunt.

Squirrels are common in our woods; grey squirrels, that is, although we see fox squirrels on occasions. When the acorns are ripe many are knocked from the trees as the squirrels scurry through the terminal limbs in their efforts to get some for themselves. Also, many of the ones they do begin to eat are dropped before completion. Deer sniff out and eat these fallen acorns and oftentimes do not arrive until after the squirrel activity has begun. This may be due to both species reacting to common cues for feeding times, but the deer show up after the patter of dropping acorns and acorn husks so often that I feel the sounds of feeding squirrels beckon them and therefore I am always pleased to have the bushytails noisily engaged near my stand.

The cries of squirrels are interesting. Two of their alarm cries are very distinct. When threatened by an aerial predator, they emit a rapid, chattering cry. This can be triggered by the sight of a hawk or owl, but also sometimes by the shadow of a bird or by owl hoots or hawk screams. Once the initial burst of chattering is over, the squirrel often emits low whines intermittently and other squirrels may answer until they feel the danger is past. Seldom do they repeat the loud chattering. Deer almost invariably ignore this cry in our swampwoods.

Predators or perceived predators on the ground or climbing trees evoke more of a barking alarm cry; typically a series of two or three barks which often are followed by the whine. If the squirrel is in a position it considers safe, it usually waves its tail concomitantly and the barking cry is repeated over and over like scolding jeers until the threat is gone. Again a whining period may succeed the alarm cries. Deer may associate these cries with danger. With enough time in the woods, one sees many interactions and I have witnessed deer spooked by these barks many times, made cautious by them even more, and totally ignore them on occasion. I'll recount two examples that are notable because in one the barks are fairly distant and in the other they unusually close.

From a tree in the swamp, but near the pasture edge, I watched a buck feed intently. He was upwind and out of bow range. For twenty minutes he fed, covering very little ground, but gradually drifting closer. He was completely at ease and seldom even raised his head. Suddenly a squirrel, probably 120 yards from me and a wee bit less from the buck, let loose a jarring series of cries denoting a predator on the ground. The buck instantly raised his head and cupped his ears toward the sound. The barks continued for what seemed like three minutes and the buck looked tense and ready to bolt for the entire duration. After the cries died, he dropped his head toward the ground once or twice as though he would resume feeding, but remained wary and ended up walking off quickly; away from the squirrel and, unfortunately, away from me as well.

Hunting from the stand described in Chapter 3 as being remarkable for how often deer failed to smell me despite the exceptionally low height of the stand, I had been entertained by the scampering antics of squirrels for over an hour and a half when one merely two yards away became suspicious. He flared his nostrils and alternated between purring snorts and sniffs, bobbing his head higher and higher. After a minute or so of this behavior, he started screaming his alarm barks and continued for what seemed a terribly long time. With dismay I assumed that the chances for deer coming into the area had diminished dramatically and night would fall within forty-five or fifty minutes. No sooner had the thought occurred than a doe and button buck ambled unconcernedly into sight. They fed on acorns around my stand for a half an hour, most of the time directly under it and for at least the first minute and possibly the first five, as interminable as it seemed, the squirrel barked and pointed at me from a few feet away. Neither deer paid the slightest attention, not even to the point of glancing up at it. By the way, one can really appreciate how loudly a squirrel barks for such a small animal from the distance of a yard or two!

Although deer seldom elicit squirrel barks, sometimes when spooked deer flee through the woods their progress is marked by the raucous sound of disturbed squirrels. Even more dismaying to squirrels is the sudden death of running deer. When blood trailing, it saves time to mark the trail and then proceed directly to their frantic cries. Every time this has happened, I found the downed deer within immediate sight of the hysterical squirrels and I know of one instance when the only reason a hunter discovered he had hit a whitetail was because of the squirrel cries.

It was another year when Ozzie and I had both drawn Tosahatchee permits and were hunting near one another. With his compound bow, he aimed at a broadside spike feeding in the vicinity with his head down and forward. The distance was greater than it appeared and Ozzie distinctly saw his arrow zip eight or so inches below the chest. A clean miss! The spike rocketed away. Disappointed, Ozzie remained on the stand hopeful of another chance before the end of the day. Sixty or seventy yards off, the squirrels had gone crazy with their cries and after this continued for several minutes, Oz decided to investigate. Below the squirrels, the young buck lie dead.

Sure of his eyes, Ozzie would not have gotten down until dark and there would be no surprise in failing to find his arrow in the swampy terrain and little further thought would have been given to the deer if not for the squirrels (except, perhaps, thoughts of how one misses easy, broadside targets). What had actually transpired is interesting as well. The far front leg of the spike was positioned forward as he fed and the near one was angled back and the head was low nibbling something as ground level. The low flying arrow grazed the bone of the near foreleg and ricocheted forward slicing one of the great blood vessels of the neck. No doubt, a grand blood trail had occurred, but it is doubtful the hunter would have known to search for it.

Incidentally, deer also become alarmed enough to sometimes snort at dead deer. I witnessed it first while sitting in a stand in sight of the fallen form of a doe I arrowed earlier. Since then, there have been several times deer snorts have alerted me to the position of a downed deer. Once I was on a good blood trail, but heard the blowing and went to take a look and found the trail's end and another time, after my shot, but before I descended from the tree, repeated blows enabled me to get a compass bearing and some trees as visual landmarks, allowing me to short cut the blood trail completely (although, like most bowhunters, I'm enough of a blood trailing nut that I was compelled to go back and solve it anyway). Deer snorts played a role in locating the deer with the severe abscess described later in Chapter 13 and the story is worth including.

From a stand in Bull Creek at one of its widest points, I spied a big doe with two grown fawns draw steadily nearer. Five yards distant, the doe stepped behind a tree. Thankful for cover the intervening trunk provided, I shifted my bow slightly, readying it for she would be in perfect position and broadside when she emerged. Except she didn't emerge. One alert ear was visible beyond the tree and, in retrospect, I concluded she had caught sight of the movement my shadow on the trees in front of her. Regardless, she bolted and was ten yards off by the time I could draw Deer Bane. I counseled myself to pick a spot and lead it and by then she was fifteen. The arrow streaked forward and drove in just in front of the hindquarters and slightly to the left (my side) of midline. She ran out of sight. The other two deer ran as well, but in a different direction.

I felt I hadn't led her enough and feared she was gut shot, but then realized the arrow should have passed completely through with only guts in its path. This thought gave me hope, but not enough hope to start trailing too soon. If it was a gut wound I did not want to push her. Forty minutes later, a snort emanated from where my last view of the doe had been and then another and a white tail bounced and waved away. There was no way a deer could have seen, heard, or smelled me so the likelihood was that it had encountered my fallen doe and, sure enough, when I got down and investigated, the doe was there. She weighed 110 pounds without her leg bones and hooves. My broadhead passed through the heart and nearly cut it in two. The tip passed far enough through the skin at the front of her chest that there was a prominent blood trail.

I find raccoons to be helpful to deer hunting in a totally different way. In our area at least, raccoons and deer have similar tastes in mast products. Our squirrels will feed on any of the acorns and their presence doesn't necessarily connote a favored tree. When one encounters raccoons feeding in a oak tree, it is a safe bet that deer also prefer those acorns. This is true of persimmons (which vary greatly in desirability to game), cabbage palm berries, oranges, and other masts. Using raccoon tastes to select deer food sources can be done from the distance and thereby limits scent contamination of the spot. Most of our wild oranges are sour and are ignored by game, even hogs, but the sweet ones are reward enough that deer routinely check the vicinity of the trees when they are dropping. It is easy enough to determine if a tree is sweet by tasting its fruit, but raccoons can provide the information when the fruit is too high to reach or when scouting from a little distance by binoculars. The raccoons eat many of the oranges in the trees, scooping out the juicy pulp and leaving the empty rind hollowed out and still hanging by its stem. These rinds wither and brown in a day or two and are ample evidence of a sweet tree and therefore a whitetail attractant. Like squirrels, raccoons knock down masts that they don't consume and the noise may draw whitetails since there is competition to reach the food among the animals which feast on the fall mast products.

Speaking of competition, hogs are worth mentioning. Deer are nervous of them and nearly always move away whenever a group of hogs approach. I once witnessed seven deer feeding under a lone oak when a boar aggressively chased them away and charged after them each time any of them returned to within even thirty yards of the tree. This oak was located in an area of cypress and pasture and few oaks. The ground under it was piled with fallen acorns. Because hogs and deer are both attracted to mast products, they are often found in proximity to one another, but rarely side by side.

Turkeys likewise favor these areas and can often be seen near deer or hogs. It has been written that deer avoid turkeys because of the noise turkeys make when scratching and feeding, but in our woods and pastures they can often be seen together basically ignoring one another except when any individual detects danger, in which case both species react to the warning, most often by fleeing.

Bobcats affect deer hunting because whitetails tend to be afraid or, at least, wary of them. One morning, from my stand in some oaks, I heard the crunch of hoof steps to the west emanating from a thick area of palmettos that were at least chest high on a man. The cause was not visible, but the noise continued and the palmetto fronds rattled occasionally as the animal pushed through them. I readied Deer Bane and waited as the steps approached. Suddenly, a deer bolted from the patch and bounded to the south. At sixty yards it turned and snorted shrilly several times back at the patch. As I contemplated how it could possibly have discerned me with the wind in my favor and the fronds blocking its view, a bobcat casually strolled out of the palmettos. The deer blew again and raced away.

A friend watched excitedly as a buck strode along a trail that led near his stand. Where the trail passed below a horizontal branch of a pine tree, the buck halted abruptly and began stamping. After more nervous stamping and a few little false jumps backwards, the deer walked back the way it had come and then entered the thick woods. My friend was puzzled because the deer was upwind, he wasn't in a direct line of sight, and he had remained still. A good while later, a movement on the pine branch drew his attention. A large bobcat was perched on the branch and was easily seen now that he knew it was there, but it had been indistinguishable all morning.

Bobcat characteristics are enjoyable to study in the swampwoods; the silent steps, the tendency to travel along logs whenever possible, and the alert and curious nature. Two examples of this curiosity are worth including. Many years ago, as a prize in an archery shoot, I was given some fox urine and, willing to experiment, carried it with me hunting. One afternoon in the dense greenery of a tangled cypress head, a bobcat slipped in silently. I say 'slipped in', but, in truth, walked in nonchalantly. A bobcat can sneak unbelievably well (as demonstrated around some of my turkey decoys), but most often they walk about seemingly unconcerned. It is just the silence of their approach that lends the atmosphere of stealth. This one climbed a slightly elevated log, stretched out and licked his fur for a while and then appeared to nap. The wind was from me to him, but caused the cat no alarm either from currents carrying my scent up or from the lack of sensitivity of his nose. I have often heard and read of bobcats' weak sense of smell and this may have been an example, but I must add that there have been times they scented me and in a page or two you will find further evidence of their olfactory abilities. This time, after fifteen or twenty minutes of the cat sleeping ten yards away, I thought of the fox urine and became curious how he would react. When a few drops had splattered down below my stand, the bobcat stood and scanned that area. Then, stretching his neck, he padded down the log and stood below me poking his nose to the ground and to the surrounding vegetation. His inquisitiveness was obvious, but was brought to an abrupt halt by a couple of the drops landing on his head and neck. He shot back several feet and then strode briskly away turning his head twice with looks that could be of puzzlement or could possibly be glares.

During a hot and mosquitoey afternoon hunt in the Bull Creek swamp bottom, a bobcat emerged from some palmettos and intently studied the trunks of several cabbage palms even scanning up their height apparently for squirrels. It was still broad daylight, but under the dense canopy of the swamp and with the dark color of the forest floor, there was not sufficient light for a shutter speed fast enough to effectuate a decent photograph. Because this was the usual case, my camera was armed with a speedlight flash. This flash caught the bobcat's attention on the first shot and after the second exposure he raced to my tree and stared up. I took two exposures of him at the base of the tree and then he climbed three or four feet up, jumped down and scudded away.

While the immediate presence of a bobcat may make deer uncomfortable, their scent does not seem to deter deer from an area, at least not always. On a few occasions, I've seen deer use a trail a bobcat had used only an hour or so before. In fact, one time a bobcat trotted through the woods past my tree stand and was barely out of sight when a second cat emerged and followed the first one's course between the trees and palmetto clumps apparently by scent despite their reputation for having poor noses. In the next couple hours, five different deer passed through the region intercepting the bobcat route at various points and none of the deer displayed the least sign of alarm.

While not wildlife, cattle share many of the lands on which I hunt and definitely can have an affect on deer hunts. Firstly, they have tendency to run away from a stalking hunter in whatever direction the person is heading. This, of course, is what makes it easy for one or two people to drive and control a small herd, but it can be frustrating to the still hunter as cattle behind one will actually run ahead to then be ready to repeatedly gallop off whichever way the stalker tries to go. The noise they make is tremendous even when only one or two are stampeding, hooves pounding heavily on the ground and large bodies crashing through brush and palmettos, and most often there will be fifteen to forty of them because once one starts to run, every cow nearby wants to join the stampede. After attaining a safe distance, they will turn around and note one's progress and when the progress becomes sufficiently close, they thunder off again. This chain of events can keep going forty-five minutes or more and with their loudness and their distraught behavior, there is little chance of any game being left undisturbed. Bulls are not nearly as bad and are much easier to stalk around or through, but there are many fewer of them than cows.

As impossible as they render still hunting with this aggravating tendency, I can recall one time cattle helped me get close to deer. The weather had been dry and desiccated leaves crackled under each foot fall making quiet movement extremely difficult. A wide trail, hedged on either side by high and thick walls of palmettos, cut below the trees, occasionally intersecting broader, grassy spaces and I was attempting to slip from one to another of these in hopes of spotting a deer. Instead I encountered eleven head of cattle and they proceeded to run noisily down the trail, stop, and crash off again. Evening was falling and if I retreated my steps the trail would restrict me to the thick and away from good stalking territory for a good portion of the remaining daylight. There was great terrain ahead and it was likely deer would venture into the pasture's edge as the day waned so I decided to walk with no attempt at stealth in the wake of the small herd and resume hunting when I reached the junction of the oaks and the pasture. Hopefully, once there, I could branch away from the cattle. I tromped loudly along the leaf strewn trail and halted abruptly where it, at long last, emptied into the open for there were two does and a spike barely thirty yards distant and totally unconcerned. My heavy crunching tread must have only seemed another cow to them. I desired a closer shot and felt a stalk would not be too chancy and it may not have been if not for the unfortunate arrival of another doe coinciding with my scampers toward a bush. Regardless, only the presence of the cows could have allowed my noisy arrival to go unnoticed by the three whitetails.

Cattle come into play on stand hunts on occasion as well. A very fine buck fed toward a stand I had placed at the intersection of two dikes that drained the surrounding rough pasture and cypress. Like the buck, the wind was coming from the north. South of the stand was an east-west fenceline and cattle were traveling along its far side. They were downwind of me and as individuals or groups would catch my scent they would stop and sniff and sniff again and look mystified. This had been going on for all morning, but now with the buck a hundred and forty or fifty yards away and unworried, the cows decided to stampede through the thick palmettos behind them. There were at least forty head and the thundering noise shattered the pleasant morning stillness and the crashing and pounding went on and on as still other cows joined in on the assumption, I suppose, that there must be a good cause for it. As one would guess, the buck was transformed into an alert and nervous statue and remained that way for an unbelievably long time. When he eventually did resume movement it was still toward me, but he no longer fed. Now he advanced in small sprints punctuated with repeated stops, his bearing tense and suspicious. His course altered as well. Instead of staying tight to the dike's hedge where he was more hidden and sheltered, but also where something could lurk unseen, he looped out into the open pasture. Obviously, he was still heading to the crossing below my stand. This stand had been impossible to reach from downwind because of the deep cypress pond behind the palmettos so rather than risk depositing scent on the dike or along the fenceline where deer were might move, I had made my predawn approach through the coverless pasture, the path that seemed least likely for a deer to encounter, but the deer's modified route intercepted my earlier path and he again froze forty yards away. He was nice buck and there was something unusual or extra about this right antler, perhaps a double main beam. Forty yards is a long way for me to confidently shoot, but I was tempted. Two considerations constrained me. First, he was as keyed up and nervous as a deer can get. Deer have ducked or jumped my arrows from as little as eleven yards so, in this instance, there was no predicting how far away and in what direction he would be when the arrow arrived. Secondly, he seemed unusually determined to reach the crossing and after the first time he was motionless, he had decided to steadfastly head that way. I hoped he would yet attempt to cross there. This proved not to be case and he bolted west and was gone.

The animals discussed in this chapter are the primary ones that have influenced my deer hunts. Obviously, other creatures can and have. Once a coyote howl spooked some deer feeding near me and sandhill cranes, common enough in our pastures and having markedly acute eyesight, have squawked their rusty alarm calls repeatedly whenever they glimpsed me still hunting, betraying my presence far and wide. Even snipe have figured into some of my hunts. There was a three week period when I consistently spotted three different bucks from a stand in a marshy region. The area was teeming with snipe and, as the deer browsed about the marsh, the birds would flush with their sporting little alarm "mreeenck!" announcing the bucks' whereabouts long before they were in view. Attention to the ways and habits of all the denizens of the swampwoods makes a more adept hunter and woodsman.

Snakes rarely figure into deer hunting here, but, for some reason, they are the creatures asked about most frequently by visiting hunters. They are part of the wilds and racers, indigos, and ribbon snakes are encountered regularly enough; red rats, yellow rats, water snakes, garter snakes, hognose snakes, coachwhips, and water moccasins now and then; and coral snakes, pigmy and diamondback rattlers, mud snakes, and king snakes only seldom. Interestingly, I typically discover more poisonous snakes in my ten or so days hunting Colorado each fall than I find here in the average year.

11

A Few Fall Turkeys

One archery season, a slightly raised area in the Bull Creek swamp bottom that held a handful of acorn laden oak trees showed tremendous deer, hog, and turkey sign. Abundant cabbage palms offered easy climbing, but in an effort to hide myself the best, I secured my stand in a peculiar maple that had two trunks that joined and separated repeatedly as they grew upwards.

The following morning, I arrived in time to watch the darkness slip farther away between the trees and witness the nocturnal vagueness of the swamp solidify into gnarled oaks, saw palmettos, and mossy trunks of cabbage palms. Turkeys called from their varied roosts and I yelped back at intervals. They seemed in no hurry to leave their perches, but finally when one glided down perhaps forty-five yards from me, the others followed suit. I had readied Deer Bane and now tried to melt further back into the confused trunk of the maple. After emitting two soft series of yelps, I remained silent and still.

Unbelievably, in single file, they headed directly toward me drawing nearer and nearer. Fearful of being discovered at any second, I searched desperately for a beard and saw only grey heads and smooth chests. When the lead hen closed to less than fifteen yards, I noted the seventh and eighth birds were bigger and darker than the others and, sure enough, sported short black beards. By now, the first hens were nearly below and the jakes fourteen or fifteen yards off. Somehow they had failed to detect me, but could I make the motions to point and draw the bow without spooking the whole flock? Knowing how quickly opportunities can evaporate, I determined to take my chances now and focusing on the closest jake's chest I picked a spot, drew and let fly an arrow. Somehow, all this motion went undetected and when the stricken bird flapped about loudly and frantically, its companions stood and stared and inclined their heads this way and that for a split second before running off as a group.

The broadhead had passed through the bird and driven into the ground. With him pinned it seemed there would be no difficulty finding him, but while this thought was comforting, it was short lived, dispelled almost immediately as his efforts pulled the arrow free of the swamp soil and away he flew careening off of cypress saplings and having difficulty attaining any altitude until the head of the arrow got caught on a thin tree that had fallen sideways. The arrow pulled free and he beat onward through the upper level of the forest unimpeded.

After a wait of thirty or forty minutes, I climbed down and searched for him. Beyond the arrow under the horizontal tree, I could find no sign at all and an hour later my hopes were very diminished. I returned to my tree. A few cut feathers gave evidence of precisely where the jake had been struck. I took a compass reading from that spot to where the arrow had fallen and walked an extension of that course. Two hundred or more yards away in an exact line lay the jake, wings spread and angled back, having died in flight.

Returning to the stand with my trophy, I photographed a spike buck that lingered nearby for a short time. He was large, but thin with a long, grey head and long, skinny neck. Incidentally, I've twice since used the compass technique to find turkeys that flew off with arrows. No doubt, it is not a hard and fast rule, but obviously a substantial percentage of mortally wounded birds fly in a beeline and it's worth a try when difficulty is encountered finding a stricken turkey.

The double-trunked tree that helped hide the author from the sharp
eyes of the turkey flock.

A different year, I set up a crotch stand in the fork of a scrubby, old oak. Lots
of leafy branches grew up around the stand and vines ran down from them
affording me concealment nearly equal to a blind, but still allowing many shooting avenues. The woods around it was swampy and full of oaks and persimmons.
The afternoon was early and hot and, reading a book and swatting mosquitoes, I
waited for the evening game movement to begin. Whether the book was that
good or my expectations of seeing animals early that low is hard to say, but obviously my alertness was not at a peak for the first indication I had of the gobblers'
presence was the light purring, clucks, and talk of feeding turkeys. Seven gobblers
were within ten yards!

Amazingly, I was able to stand, ready Simplicity, draw and miss without
spooking them. My second miss caused a little more concern and the closest gobblers eyed the arrow suspiciously, but still they were completely unaware of me.
My quiver carried five arrows, but one was tipped with only a judo point so my
third and fourth misses left me watching the nervous birds walk off in the direction from whence they came with a sense of frustration and aggravation. A thick
line of saw palmettos, like an impenetrable hedge ran east of the stand and, since
they had never discovered me, when they rounded the south end, I bolted down

from the tree, grabbed two of my poorly shot arrows and ran to the corner of the palmettos and peered around. The gobblers were right there. Drawing Simplicity again, I launched one of the arrows at the nearest bird which skewered him. He and the other birds jumped into the air and some ran and some flew away. I thought he flew to a tree twenty yards off, but couldn't find him and returned to see what my arrow would show. He was lying there, having jumped and died and my eye had confused another gobbler with him in the melee of panicked birds.

I returned to my tree, climbed it and with the bird at its base, continued to hunt. No deer showed up that evening, but twice I had to chase off raccoons that scented my gobbler and tried to drag it away. After that episode, I fashioned a small broadhead sheath and began carrying an extra broadhead in my pocket that I can exchange with my practice head if the need arises for one more arrow.

Another adventure offered insight as to why arrowed turkeys can be troublesome to find. A few years back, an elk hunt in Colorado caused me to miss the opening weekend of archery season here at home so I went out the first morning I was back. My luck went well and I arrowed a beautiful doe, but it was still early and so I decided to sit and watch, comfortable in my stand in a lone live oak in an overgrown pasture. The oak was thick and leafy and offered great concealment and I had cut tunnels through the dense foliage to afford shots in most directions. A lone jake walked up and with good fortune and my longbow Daddy, my arrow drilled him. He sped off for forty yards whereupon he entered a patch of stunted palmettos. He did not appear to leave.

An exciting hour passed during which I rattled in an incredible buck which winded me at twelve yards as he circled downwind, just eighteen or so inches shy of being in the same shooting lane as the jake had been. Getting down I walked to the palmetto clump. The jake was there, dead, but if I hadn't seen where he had gone it is unlikely I would have found him. He wedged himself headfirst into the brown, fibrous palmetto roots and made himself look skinny and long, rendering him nearly indistinguishable from his surroundings. It would be hard to imagine casually looking for him, not knowing his location and noticing his still form.

Having witnessed this behavior, I was particularly struck when reading one of Theodore Roosevelt's books by his mention of the same tendency. Here are his words. "A turkey, after coming down from his first flight, will really perform the feat which fable attributes to the ostrich; that is, will run its head into a clump of bushes and stand motionless as if, since it cannot see its foes, it were itself equally invisible."

One fall afternoon, I managed to get off of work early enough to allow a hunt. Two different areas in the Tyson Creek strand seemed to call me, each with acorns dropping and bountiful animal sign and both flavored with concentrated buck rubs. One was suited for winds of any east angle and the other for winds of any west direction. They were quite a ways apart and required entry from opposite sides of the swamp. The weather radio stated winds were currently from the north and predicted continued north winds the remainder of the day and night. Due north would work equally as well at either spot so to save time I chose the closest place.

The rain of the past few days that accompanied the cool front that, in turn, furnished the north winds had drastically raised the water level in the swamp and forced me to detour further north than I wished to reach the spot. My scent trail would not be too worrisome because the water I waded was flowing rapidly, but I spooked two does from the area and the wind was pronouncedly from the northeast! I returned to my truck having squandered forty-five minutes and still facing a fifteen minute drive and two gates. During the drive, all the cattle were feeding actively, heightening my desire to be on the stand. As I carried my stand, bow, and gear across a pasture, a group of gobblers were at the strand's edge to the north. Taking care to keep myrtles between us, I continued to the swamp woods. The turkeys were stalkable, but by now I was quite intent on getting to the stand site without much more delay, plus the stalk would get my scent over much of the area from which the game should come. Circling around some feeding hogs I reached my tree. Another group of hogs came by as I climbed. The game was moving!

Finally situated, I noted a few raccoons in a couple freshets. Ten minutes may have passed, but probably not, when ripples eighty yards north on a shallow creek indicated an animal moving. Because of many intervening trees and cabbage palms, binoculars only magnified the ripples without revealing their cause, but then at forty-five yards when the "sploosh sploosh" sounds of steps were audible, the stilt-like legs and swinging beard of a big Osceola became visible. It was followed by another and others still. They were striding purposefully my way and if they fed at all it was so quickly and occasionally that I didn't notice. Thankful for the screening tree trunks, I readied Bane Too. The birds were close now with the lead gobbler behind a cabbage palm trunk. I drew. Passing the tree, he was in the open and I had a fifteen yard shot at him, front on. Expecting to be discovered at any instant, I dared not wait to compare him to the other birds, but let the heavy arrow drive. He jumped, wrenching the broadhead from the ground, raced about twelve yards flapping twice, and fell dead in the creek. The arrow had entered the base of his neck and exited the vent. Even more amazingly, the other gobblers had been behind the screen of trees and now were 'pucking' and stepping nervously, bewildered by the strange behavior of one of their group. I managed to hang my bow and man my videocamera while they 'pucked' and gawked, stretching their necks over the nearly sunken body and cocking their heads. At last they departed uneasily.

The gobbler was huge and had nice spurs. His beard was only nine inches, but was exceptionally thick and ropey.

Once, walking with Bane Too and scouting for deer sign during some midday hours, I crossed an open area of short grass and saw a brown lump resembling a large and oblong cow patty. Passing by it at ten to thirteen yards, a second glance that astonished me revealed it was a grand gobbler laying nestled flat against the ground with its neck outstretched and its hard, little eye glittering. There was no cover anywhere nearby and thereby no reason that I should have surprised the bird and caused him to hide where there was nothing to hide him. It seemed he should have spied me at a good distance and run so I was skeptical of my good fortune and failed to nock an arrow even when he allowed me to step within four yards, believing he had to be sick or injured. Three yards proved too close for him to tolerate and he ran with a healthy gobbler's speed, dispelling any notion of infirmity and exceeding the range of my arrows before I could string one and draw the bow. Feeling phenomenally foolish, I couldn't help remembering hunting with my dad and finding a good boar hog laying in the sun on a cold morning. "Shoot it!" I urged since my dad had professed a desire for a hog earlier the very same morning, but he said it must be dead. The hog's flanks moved barely, but regularly as it breathed so I encouraged him to shoot again. Still unconvinced, my dad approached closer, within scant yards and told me again that it must be dead. I had stayed back a bit and Dad had to raise his voice to tell me this. The hog responded by getting groggily to its feet and looking like I feel when aroused from a comfortable, deep nap. My dad watched as the boar looked about. Then, shaking his heavy, black head, the hog dashed away. Curious, I queried why Dad hadn't drawn when the hog stood up and proved it was not dead.

"I thought it must be sick."

Now, several years later I missed an opportunity because of the same doubts.

12

Charged Action

Hunters hear frequently of the aggressiveness of wild boars, but even with arrowing or spearing countless hogs from close range on the ground, I've been lucky enough to have never had one immediately attack me. A few times hogs ran into or near me by coincidence as they sought to flee and several times I've witnessed arrowed hogs vent their instantaneous rage on a nearby hog or tree. Their anger is quick and intense. One large boar broke the arrow I had driven into his chest off on a neighboring boar and pummeled him savagely with head and tusks. The oppressed boar ran off squealing submissively and the big boar strutted about and then collapsed dead.

The only occasions I've actually faced full-hearted charges occurred when following up wounded hogs. In the open with good visibility, this is not very troublesome for a hunter can usually out run or dodge the attack (more easily, if the hunter is accompanied by friends like mine, than he can dodge the gleeful laughter and merriment that accompanies the charge). Sometimes it is not quite as simple. Interestingly, my closest calls were not extraordinarily large hogs and one was a sow.

With the evening sun low in the sky and beginning to redden, snapping palm fronds and sticks manifested the presence of hogs on the edge of the swamp. Minutes passed without the sounds getting appreciably nearer my perch deep within the creek bottom and with no more than fifty minutes of light left, I decided to attempt a stalk. I packed up my camera, flash, and other gear and climbed down from the stand.

Leaving the pack behind, I traversed a couple sloughs and managed to slip in near them. Several were close at hand and a good sized one was eight yards off, quartering away. Two smaller ones were a tad closer and I watched, incredulous that they hadn't smelled me with the light wind, trying to decide if I wanted to try for the biggest one. She turned toward me and rooted with her head down and another smaller hog ran up and started rooting less than a yard from my boots. With probably only a few seconds until I'd be discovered, I decided to shoot and, aiming at the largest hog with the broadhead's back edge against my finger and Deer Bane's handle comfortable in my hand, I let the arrow go which struck with a heavy thunk. The sow went down and rolled.

The other hogs raced and milled about, but none left the area being uncertain what happened. Then the wounded sow got up and ran and they all followed. I had a flashlight in my pack, but that was back at the base of my tree. I considered returning for it because with the fading light blood trailing would be difficult or impossible, but I could hear the hogs ahead and decided not to waste the time and followed them by ear.

It sounded as though she had stopped outside of the swamp, but once there I heard crashing sounds in a small head. Then more grunts and noises led me beyond the head into a pasture. It turned out that there were fifteen black hogs none of which were piglets or small shoats. Unsure if maybe I had passed her in the poor light, I elected to press on chasing the hogs' sounds and silhouettes because if I was to blood trail now I'd have to return to the very start and I had covered a few hundred yards.

The hogs did not resume feeding and each time I reached the locale of the last rustling or grunting, I would have to wait and listen and take after them again. After another three or four hundred yards, I could see three hogs walking in front of me. Then I saw in the partial moonlight (the daylight was now utterly gone) a big hog to my right. I drew close to see if it was wounded and it bellowed and wheeled off apparently unharmed. This increased the nervousness of the three hogs, so as I attempted to catch back up with them, they bolted, but the largest one seemed to lag slightly so I nocked an arrow and let fly, but the sound of the hit was only that of an arrow zipping through grass and dog fennels. The other two hogs poured it on and left her far behind. She had to be the one.

Ahead loomed another dark strand of swamp finger and fearing the likelihood of losing her in its shadows, I dashed ahead of her hoping to herd her back from it. Happily, although not the safest course, I had pulled another arrow from my quiver. Suddenly, she charged toward me as fast as any hog I'd seen, rejuvenated with desperation! Frightened, I slipped the arrow on the string, drew and let go when she was no more than four feet from me and coming fast. The arrow drove down through one ear, her neck, and her chest. The force of its entry staggered her, but her momentum carried her forward. I was trying to run backwards at this time. The lighting was very poor and this black hog lunging wildly at me with its head twisted and ready to rip and slash was very startling. She fell, raised up and made it two yards and fell again. When I later cleaned her I learned the initial arrow had been stopped by her massive backbone and the point had never reached the chest cavity.

In a different year, but in actuality not terribly far from where the sow fell, I happened upon a lone boar hog. The pasture was overgrown where he was rooting, but this gave me good cover and allowed an easy stalk. With the boar broadside, my arrow struck the shoulder and he ran off with only a quarter of the fletching end of the arrow protruding from the wound. He fled into a big patch of briars, grapevine, and greenbrier. With a broadside shoulder shot and that much penetration, his death was but seconds off.

I waited a minute or two or maybe three and proceeded to traipse to the viney thicket. Once there I was surprised to find less blood than I expected, but it was still followable and so I followed where the briars and vines allowed and detoured and intercepted it as necessary. All at once, the hog I thought was dead came at me in a mad rush from just feet away. I turned to run, but the vines got my feet and I was down. I couldn't get back up and I could hear the hog at my feet with repeated short grunts that all flowed together like a rhythmically accentuated vicious growl. The whole time his teeth were popping and clacking as well and I anticipated feeling them at any instant. Abandoning my bow, I attempted to crawl, but as desperately and wildly as my limbs struggled, I made only slight headway, the clutching vines and briars impeding any progress. I could hear him inches from me and thereby did not really feel the briars. When I finally regained my feet, I looked back and saw that my arrow, point end protruding from his neck, had hooked under many vines and they held him like a harness and they had encumbered him enough to allow me a graceless and drawn out escape.

His desire to attack me remained ardent and I utilized it to draw him away from my bow and when he was far enough I returned for it. Even with the bow, I had a hard time getting a good shot opportunity because of the closeness of the thicket and because of his steadfastness in facing me head on. At long last, I circled enough to work him broadside and dispatched him.

It turned out that when my original arrow hit his shoulder, the broadhead bent badly and curled forward and the arrow, following it, turned and went out the neck without reaching the chest so while I thought it had to be a double lung shot with that much penetration, in truth it was a flesh wound. What's more, the hog was under a hundred pounds.

My face, ears, arms, and hands were scratched a bit and bleeding. When my friends asked me about it, I just told them I was attacked by a hog. Of course, it didn't take them long to get the whole story out of me and some of them still chuckle about it.

13

Unusual Deer

With enough time in the woods and around game, a sportsman is certain to be exposed to a few oddities and over the years some have come to my view. None of them are profoundly remarkable, but they may be of interest to other lovers of whitetails and nature.

A seven and a half year old doe I managed to arrow late one season was missing her lower left first molar and her lower right first molar appeared to have hair growing from the gums around it. Hair growth in the mouth is highly exceptional in most mammals, so I desired to investigate further. The jaw was swollen beneath the molar and it was quite loose in its socket because of a pronounced loss of surrounding bone. I wrote in my notes at the time: "So tremendous was the bone loss that upon first inspection and even after the jaw was boiled and cleaned it appeared that hair was growing out of the jaw around the tooth." This proved to be plant fibers from food materials forced into the swollen space between tooth and gums and only those fibers that aligned vertically would be thus impacted. This alignment of fibers explains the parallel, brown, hair-like tufts. The gums and bone had withdrawn from the tooth all the way past the depths of its roots and so these impacted fibers extended nearly an inch into the jaw bone. The roots of the tooth had a moth-eaten appearance that indicates the doe's own cells were trying to resorb it. In addition, a hole had formed in the swollen portion of the mandible offering another avenue of drainage.

Earlier in the book I mentioned a buck with another abscessed molar. In both cases, the infection looked swollen and painful, and anyone who has had a small bit of food material, say a piece of popcorn husk, caught under the gums for a day or so can imagine the stoicism of these animals as they continue to feed and live.

Deer Jaw with Abscessed Molar Tooth

A. A fistula or hole through the bone allowing the infection to drain. B. The moth eaten appearance of both the bone and the root surfaces. This tooth was quite loose in the socket. Close inspection of the photograph reveals a major crack running completely through the tooth from its forward portion to its most distal.

The whitetail deer's hardiness is also evidenced by a doe I saw several times during one fall and winter in the company of four other does. She walked with a limp, but always kept up with the others even on the occasions when they caught my scent and raced away. I held one doe tag throughout the season so my dad could be free to try for any deer that allowed him a shot, but with the advent of the last weekend, decided to use it if a chance presented and this limping doe was the first to amble within bow range. The source of her limp became obvious upon cleaning her. The joint of her front left leg to the shoulder just above the level of the bottom of the chest was displaced laterally so that the two cartilage coated bone ends did not meet and the weight was transmitted simply by the capsule of the joint. The bones themselves overlapped at least an inch and I suspect she had lived with the injury for a long while because each of the two bones was worn where they overlapped about a quarter of the way through. Her weight and condition as evidenced by kidney fat were normal for our does and she appeared normal and healthy in all other regards.

Another anomaly showed up cleaning a different doe and I'm still puzzled over it. The deer approached loudly along a creek so I was ready even though the vegetation, incredibly thick, obscured a decent view of her until she was below me and my arrow caught her. She retreated the way she approached so, unfortunately, I never got to witness how she walked or ran. Halfway down the flesh of her hams, her main muscles were completely segmented horizontally from the back of the muscle all the way to the bone. Both legs were identical. The segments were encased in fascia and while the segments were flat as though sliced by a knife, the corners were rounded and smooth. The hide gave no evidence of cuts or scars on the back of the legs. The hams were normal in size and development other than this tremendous peculiarity although it is difficult to conceive how they functioned, but apparently the fascia served to connect the two muscle portions although that assumption is somewhat tenuous for there was no difficulty separating these portions with just a finger once they were skinned and normal muscle contractions should exert much greater force then my finger. No fibrous scar tissue was present.

There is another occurrence that won't strike southern hunters as out of the ordinary, but may surprise others. It is the preponderance of liver flukes. Often these flukes reach two or three inches in length and come close to the diameter of a little finger. Perhaps it is worth relating a humorous incident involving them.

As mentioned earlier, on some hunts on public land the game commission requests hunters to bring their deer whole to the check station and allow the biologist to survey the condition and collect parasite samples. Once when I was checking in or out, a successful hunter was watching the biologist dress his deer and repeated three times that he wanted the liver. The game commission employee nodded and a minute or two later plopped the big organ on a bench saying nothing, but quickly making long, shallow incisions with his knife tip in several areas of the liver that looked blackish, puffy, and scarred. He returned to his work, but someone watching soon called everybody's attention to the liver by saying, "Eeeuw, it's moving!"

It was. Two of the places where the slits had been cut were bulging and contracting, pulsing in an irregular and eerie manner. Slowly big liver flukes began to emerge. The hunter watched without saying anything, but when the biologist asked if he was sure he wanted the liver he had changed his mind.

Another variation in deer is in their coloring. Piebald deer each seem unique, but are rare on our hunting grounds. Most whitetails have a white throat patch under their chin, but sometimes a deer will have none and other times two. An eight point buck with heavy tines, some exceeding eleven inches, that frequented the scrub forest we call the Peanut Farm had no change of color under his chin or on his throat and the buck described in Chapter 1 had more of a creamy than white throat shield. White eye patches are common in our deer, but some deer have eyes surrounded only by brown hair. Likewise, between the grey or brown facial hair and the black nose there may or may not be a band of white. A doe I arrowed had very dark grey fur on her chest from the back edge of her forelegs forward up her neck about eleven inches. It was much darker and greyer than the brown of her body or any other hair on her. She also had a concave chest so at mid-line her chest went back up; her sternum was elevated rather than being the lowest portion of her chest.

One December, I discovered an area in the Bull Creek swamp bottom that was teeming with wildlife. On average, ten deer could be spotted each sit and while not always within bow range, not terribly distant either as the view was fairly limited. In addition, otters, wood ducks, raccoons, squirrels, kingfishers and more entertained me and my efforts to capture some of them on film caused each episode on the stand to be busy and eventful. A nice eight point had ventured nearby twice and a group of seven does paraded about most days. Hogs and turkeys used the area as well.

One afternoon, I assumed the seven does were present at about 2:30 because of multiple partial glimpses of deer about eighty yards distant and it proved to be the case. They fed off and then back to within forty yards and then away again. About 4:45, one of the smaller does came near me. Her nose was long and mature, but she seemed little. I concluded that it was just because some of her companions were tremendously huge. She ambled down a shallow creek channel a spare couple of yards behind my tree and was sure to catch my wind any second. Pointing Moon Sliver, I pulled the string until the bow indeed resembled a crescent moon and, releasing, marveled at the near silence of the bow. The arrow flew perfectly and the doe lunged away and was rapidly lost to sight.

Tommy had crafted the bow for me and it was a joy to shoot. This was my first attempt to hunt deer with it and my worry was penetration for the bow wasn't exceptionally fast and only pulled 54 pounds. My concern proved warranted for the fletchings hadn't slipped from sight with the hit and the unimbedded portion of the shaft slapped limbs and palm fronds noisily with her frantic withdrawal. I picked out a distinctive tree from the area of the last sounds of her flight. The other does were still feeding fifty yards off and I detested spooking and thereby educating them so I waited and hoped they would wander off once more. By 5:00 the knowledge of darkness arriving within an hour and the likelihood of a poor blood trail persuaded me to climb down regardless of their presence and, with good fortune and stealth, I did so without alarming the deer.

Through the swamp her running tracks, kicked up mud, and three minuscule droplets of blood allowed me to follow her course, but where the doe exited the creek bottom, no sign was evident and I was left to explore each and every possible route. One such avenue led to a fence line and two neighboring strands of barbed wire held huge wads of deer hair. Reasoning only a desperate deer would cross through the fence so recklessly, I searched from the trail under the fence on and all the trails that branched from it. No further sign could be found and logic dictated that she could not have made it far. Chastising myself for electing to hunt with such a weak bow when I had plenty of faster and more powerful ones from which to choose, I decided to return to the last tracks in the mud of the swamp. In a hurry because of the impending twilight, I took the most direct route and crossed the fence east of the trail. Twenty or so more steps and there she was. The arrow had entered high on the chest, of course, with shooting down at a deer so close and with no exit wound, she had left no real blood trail. However, she had died quickly, flopping over and to the side just as she made it to the swamp's edge and never reaching the fence. The giant clumps of hair in the fence's barbs were only coincidental and not hers. My earlier steps had passed within nine yards of her still form.

The reason I mention her here is because she had the most peculiar body shape I've ever seen. She was incredibly short and compact from neck to tail, but much thicker than normal from left to right. Her legs were normal in length, but appeared long because they were so close together. The result was that she looked profoundly out of proportion and everyone at camp commented on it. One person likened her to a short-necked, miniature giraffe. Her teeth indicated she was three and a half years old and she weighed just under ninety pounds.

14

Hunting Lore

Being from an area that is so unlike most of those written about in hunting magazines or books drives home the realization that things a student of nature and hunting has repeatedly witnessed and accepts as factual may not be the same in a different region or under different conditions. Here there are no crop fields and often feeding and bedding areas are one and the same. The rut is not as intense, but much more prolonged, decidedly too long to be linked to a single full moon. Deer populations may be at risk from elevated water levels, but never from deep snow or cold weather. There are no ridges or hollows and definitely no shortage of water. Winds may vary as the air over the land heats up or cools compared with the more consistent temperature of the air over the ocean's waters, but there are no hills for the wind to blow up or down. Although we find occasional shed antlers, seldom is the outcome predictable in the dense vegetation and months could be spent unsuccessfully searching for them. The list of such differences could go on and on, but the point is that much that is published about deer hunting is not accurate or not applicable here and that makes me well aware that the principles and concepts that shape and guide my hunting practices and that I accept as valid may not hold true everywhere and under all conditions. Nonetheless, while it is doubtful all of anyone's hunting practices and beliefs will be universally helpful and accurate, some insights may be gleaned from the experiences of others even if the setting and conditions vary so the following is an outline sketching some of my hunting methodology.

In deer hunting, my first concern is scent. Wind direction, stand site and stand height, hygiene practices, approach to the stand or still hunting route, clothing and equipment are all involved. I've already alluded to the inconstant nature of air movement. A gust from the north that is centered to the area just east of a stand, will likely produce a current that drags scent to the west. A moment later, the scent will be carried south again and later still, if a gust now hammers down west of the stand, may then be ushered east. In the same north wind, a stand set on the south side of a dense woods with open pasture to the south will experience some air flow to the south, but also some suck-back to the north somewhat akin to the low pressure behind a moving vehicle that racecar drivers utilize when they draft. Earlier in the book, I mentioned the extreme number of scent rich skin particles that are shed by people (and mammals and birds in general) continually. Varying winds can scatter these cells in several directions around a hunter's stand as well as carry his scent directly to approaching game. These distributed particles then can provide deer or other game olfactory clues to a hunter's presence.

Understanding the air movement and possible air movement helps the hunter select the best stand locations. One area I attempted to hunt through the years because of the rich accumulation of deer sign it consistently vaunted proved frustrating beyond belief. If the shape of the woods was studied on an aerial photograph, it would closely resemble a capital letter 'H' with the desirable spot directly at the center of the cross-bar. All the areas surrounding the creekwood strands that formed the letter itself were open pasture and any gust or change of pressure in one pasture would alter the air flow about the hot spot. Typically, deer feed and cover ground at a gradual pace and, nearly invariably, before one would work close enough to afford a twenty or less yard shot, the air currents would bear them warnings of my presence. Eventually I switched tactics and set stands to intercept deer heading to the place. These new stand sites sported less sign, but provided more opportunities because the wind patterns were more stable and predictable.

When a promising place is discovered, before hanging a stand or choosing a stand location, it is prudent to consider the wind conditions in which the spot will be hunted. Thought can be given then to not only the stand site, but also to the approach to the stand. I ponder the wind and its possible eddies carefully. Hunters using a rifle or shotgun or who can shoot a bow accurately at more distant targets may succeed with less meticulous planning, but paying heed to all aspects of scent dispersal can do no harm and may prove beneficial. Who can say when a small buck may traipse haphazardly close to a stand while a larger one lags back out of range or behind cover? Most hunters have had this or something similar happen at some point and, if attention to detail prevented the small buck from spooking and thereby alarming the other buck, are glad of their efforts.

Other considerations in picking the ideal site for a stand are the vantage, the available shooting avenues, and concealment. For bowhunting especially, it is advantageous to see game early to allow the hunter time for movement or preparation and this movement is also made less obtrusive if the selected site provides some cover or at least some background. In most cases, as the height a stand is placed increases, the amount of scent reaching the ground diminishes and the less likely the hunter will be discovered by a deer's nose. Of course, trees sway and bend, and this motion is magnified with distance from the ground, at times to the point of making aiming more troublesome. Another drawback to excessive height, at least for hunting archers, is a diminution of the target. Because of the angle, the area an arrow can strike and pierce the vitals becomes smaller as the altitude of the archer becomes greater. Exit wounds are of the utmost importance to ensure a readable blood trail. While probably not a concern for hunters with modern compound bows, archers with less powerful bows may wish to contemplate that the higher the stand from which an arrow is launched, the further the broadhead must penetrate a broadside deer to provide an exit wound. (See diagrams.)

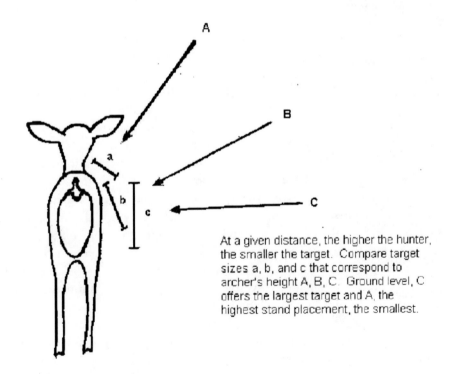

At a given distance, the higher the hunter, the smaller the target. Compare target sizes a, b, and c that correspond to archer's height A, B, C. Ground level, C offers the largest target and A, the highest stand placement, the smallest.

Shriking Dimension of Vital Area With Increased Height

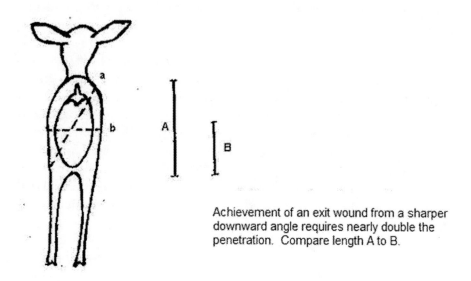

Achievement of an exit wound from a sharper downward angle requires nearly double the penetration. Compare length A to B.

Increasing Need for Penetration with Increased Height

The continual and multitudinous release of skin particles is the primary cause of our scent trail. There is a persistent perception that the scent trail arises from the leather of a hunter's boots or chemicals on his or her soles and while these could easily contribute to a scent trail, their elimination will not eliminate the scent trail. A deer, rabbit, or turkey has no leather boots nor chemically contaminated soles yet the bloodhound that can follow a man could also handily trail any of them. The shed skin cells and the oils of skin and the bacteria that accompany both are the greatest portion of our trails. Understanding this allows the hunter to devise ways of minimizing this invisible trail. Before expanding on these ways, let me clarify, lest my earlier words mislead anyone, I do wear rubber boots and strive to keep them away from any non-natural contaminants. I would not pump gas or walk into a restaurant in my boots and I'm even careful not to walk across cattle guards at midline for fear of oil leaked from vehicles.

Body oils are left in our wake whenever uncovered skin touches vegetation or other material, say a fence post or wires. This is of significant interest because it generally occurs above the level of the ground and thereby closer to the level of a deer's nose. Not that deer never have their heads near the ground for they often do, but much of the time, particularly when walking, their heads are higher. Many times when the vegetation was low, I've witnessed deer cross my trail with no visible sign of recognition, but it is rare indeed for a hog, with its nose at ground level while walking, to pass by my trail unaware. Reduction of the oil smear portion of the trail is effectuated by reducing skin contact with anything on or along the path. Clean, scent free clothing provides a barrier between the skin and vegetation. Also, a conscious effort to avoid touching obstacles is worthwhile. Ducking or circumnavigating a leafy branch and thereby preventing any scent deposition is ideal, but moving the branch by touching only one small area would still be preferable to brushing past it and smearing oil over many of its leaves. When a choice is available, the most open pathway will help reduce the body oil portion of one's trail.

Clothing is also the best method to reduce the deluge of microscopic skin particles. The particles are tiny enough to pass through cloth unless the weave is quite tight or multiple layers exist. Shirts that are tucked in catch the particles released from the torso. Long sleeve shirts with tight fitting cuffs restrict the release of particles from the arms and shoulders more than short sleeve shirts. Pants that tuck into boots catch most of cells shed from the legs thereby reducing the number that can litter one's trail. This may be the mechanism for the main advantage of rubber boots.

Cold weather bears three scent related advantages for the hunter. A whitetail's nose functions less effectively in cold, the hunter's increased clothing restricts passage of a greater portion of the skin particles, and the warm, scent laden air surrounding the hunter rises.

In days gone by, some native Americans used another method that reduced the constant rain of skin particles. Fats were rubbed into the skin. Of course, this increased the oil smear potential, but the greasy layer bound the dead and shedding skin cells and prevented them from dispersing. With careful attention to contact with vegetation, their scent trail diminished.

Anyone who has been around hunting dogs has probably heard the expression, "rain freshens the scent," meaning the scent trail is enhanced rather than diminished by rainfall. The mechanism behind this is also worth considering. Obviously skin oil is involved in the smear trail a hunter leaves, but the dead skin particles are likewise saturated with this oil as well. Deer noses (and ours, too) function by molecules traveling through the air and landing on receptors that, in turn, signal the brain that the particular scent is present. For this to happen, the molecules must first leave the scent bearing material. Several factors affect how readily these molecules escape the skin particle or oil smear and the two most important are temperature and surface area. The greater the temperature, the more active the molecules and this is one component of a deer's heightened olfaction in warmer weather. (The other concerns the deer's nose itself.) The role of surface area makes sense as well. If the molecules are all wadded into a ball, the only ones that could launch into the air to eventually reach a deer's nose are the ones on the outer surface of the ball. However, if the same molecules were spread out flat and wide and only one molecule deep, all molecules would have a chance of breaking free into the air. When water contacts our skin oil, the oil spreads out like a drop or two of gasoline spreads out over a wide expanse of water. The surface area is thus maximized and "the scent is freshened."

Incidentally, describing a molecule triggering a receptor, introduced another item of interest. Receptors are specific and can be activated by only the appropriate molecule. Whitetail noses differ from ours by having not only drastically more receptors (at least 2000% more), but also by having more types of receptors. The point is that with receptors totally alien to us, deer can detect molecules that have no odor to a human. Manufacturers and suppliers often use the description "odorless" and one must wonder, "odorless to whom?"

Bacteria in the soil break down the components of our scent trail fairly readily. Recently, I read an excellent book on using dogs to find wounded deer. The author was extremely knowledgeable and the book was full of useful and interesting information. He touted tracking dogs' abilities over aromatic terrain like cedars and fallen leaves and even asserted that skunk spray does not mask a scent trail enough to prevent a dog from following it, but, when faced with the difficulty they encounter tracking over freshly plowed soil, he surprisingly attributed the problem to the trail being masked by the abundance of earth scent instead of recognizing the effect of soil bacteria. While these bacteria are hindrances to tracking dogs, they are beneficial to hunters desirous of leaving as little and short-lived a trail as possible and wherever the ground is naked, be it sand, mud, recently washed bottom from receding waters, or a tilled fire break, the scent will linger for a much shorter duration although the effectiveness will vary with bacterial concentration. Moister soils harbor and grow more bacteria and therefore reduce a scent trail more readily and more completely. Arid, desert-like sand offers fewer soil bacteria. Obviously, freshly tilled soil will teem with bacteria and is ideal for breaking down a hunter's scent trail. One word of caution, if the soil is so moist that puddles are present, scent particles will float on the water and be less exposed to the bacteria.

An approach to the stand from downwind of the stand site is always ideal. Ranking the type of route to minimize a scent trail starting with the best, I would list them as: flowing water, raw or exposed earth, dead leaf covered earth, and short grass. As the vegetation height increases, the route becomes less and less desirable. Stagnant, nonflowing water holds the scent better than soil and usually longer than short grass. Other factors affect scent retention in addition to the substrate itself. These include wind, humidity, and temperature changes. Wind disperses and thereby dilutes the scent particles hunters leave behind. Strong winds that persist over time will diminish a scent track much more markedly than light intermittent winds. Drier air likewise reduces the detectability of a scent trail. As temperatures increase, the scent molecules become more active and are more readily discerned initially, but then as the warm air rises, it carries the scent with it and erodes the scent track.

Walking in the gently flowing water of the swamp.

It should be mentioned that while rain increases the available scent this is true only to a point after which continued rain begins to wash away and remove scent traces. Also, after a rain or dew that freshened a trail dries completely, the scent becomes more ephemeral.

These days, so much is written about keeping clothes scent free and clean, avoiding aromatic hygiene products, and reducing the scents a hunter's bows, stands, and other gear may convey, that there is no need to enlarge upon these topics here. Suffice it to say that minimizing scent is beneficial and worthwhile. In preparation for writing this book, I reviewed old journal entries and magazine articles I had penned and a statement written twenty years ago offers testimony to how firmly I adhere to a doctrine of eliminating any foreign odors. Once I wrote that despite the increase in scent level due to mosquito repellant, the bottom line was that one couldn't hunt without blood in one's veins. However, four years later, sixteen years ago, on a mosquito filled opening day of archery season, a deer blew at me and that was the last time I've applied insect repellant in deer season.

A lot of the information presented discussed aspects of human scent fairly specifically, but it may be helpful to list some of its predominate components. Our sebacious glands produce oils that lubricate and protect our skin. The outermost layer of our skin is composed of several levels of dead and compressed skin cell that are constantly resupplied from below. The collapsed and empty cells of the topmost layer fragment and are shed or are shed whole. They have absorbed the sebaceous oils and also are fertile supporters of legions of bacteria. Perspiration is moisture released by us to regulate temperature and, stemming originally from blood, contains chemicals from our bodies including salts. It has an odor itself, but fresh cooling sweat is not nearly as malodorous as aged sweat. The sweat of fear is different and has more of a reek initially. Perspiration provides a moist environment where bacteria can flourish and this is the difference between aged and fresh sweat. Bacteria are very capable odor producers and inhabit the fragmenting and shedding skin particles, the skin itself, the oil layer, perspiration, and perspiration dampened clothing.

Lungs function to exchange gases and, of course, this trades air with an increased level of carbon-dioxide for outside air with lesser levels and at the same time trades air with diminished oxygen levels for the normal percentage of nearly twenty percent. Less obvious is that anything with a greater percentage in the body than in the air will be released at the same time. Intestinal gas, the chemical constituents of spicy foods, and alcohol all are picked up by the bloodstream and when the blood courses through the lungs are set free into the air and this adds another component to human scent. The exhaled air passes through the mouth and nose and can pick up additional odors there. Not surprisingly, these odors are also released by bacteria. (Bacteria must rank among the stinkiest living things per unit weight!) The mouth has more places to harbor bacteria and therefore contaminates the released breath more. However, to a treestand hunter it may be of interest to recognize that air expended through the nose is directed downward. In cold weather the warmth of the expired air coupled with the latent heat of condensation will overcome its initial momentum after a distance determined by the force of expiration and the difference in temperatures, but in warm weather, the scent continues downward a substantial ways. Examined more closely, human scent is more complicated and multifaceted that one might think.

When still hunting, the wind is critical as well. Heading directly into the wind works well, but then the returning leg of the hunt is almost a waste. With a little forethought, a route that angles into the wind will allow the entire circuit to offer some chance of success.

Over the years, there were many times I stumbled on deer sign so tremendously abundant and fresh that it filled me with confidence that a stand set there would assuredly offer a chance at a deer. Not only would my hopes not come to fruition, but no new droppings or tracks could be found. The deer had abandoned the locale because of my intrusion and, obviously, scent had been the betraying factor. Other times, of course, my set ups worked well, but the occasions when setting a stand had radically influenced the deer's use of an area caused me concern that even when a site provided some opportunities, it may have had an even greater potential if not for scent left from my incursions into it, particularly potential for mature, hunter-wise bucks. Seldom had good bucks caught wind of me and ever returned to be viewed again from the same set up. These early experiences shaped my habits for scouting and when placing stands, making me loath the notion of leaving olfactory evidence.

Several practices have helped me minimize such traces when scouting and most of them are applicable to placing stands as well. Surveillance from the distance allows the scouter to narrow down travel patterns, corridors, and feeding sites. This can be accomplished from a remotely place stand with a good pair of binoculars to pinpoint places precisely. Binoculars are aids also for scanning trees for mast products and the ground and saplings for sign without treading too deeply into a promising zone. Scouting quite a bit ahead of time can reveal trees that will produce mast and where deer are likely to feed before they begin and any scent deposited will have ample time to fade. I attempt to perform as much reconnaissance as possible from the confines of the creeks of flowing water or from exposed soil, utilizing binoculars as described above. Vegetation holds the scent longer than earth and it is often closer to nostril level when deer pass so it is best to do the utmost to avoid contacting it. Sometimes our rains are predictable, especially later in the season when cold fronts pass, and preceding heavy or prolonged rains, I try to scout as much territory as possible.

People often ask specifically what sign should be found to consider an area the right place to hunt. This is a difficult question to answer because of the many variables. A lot of tracks could mean that a couple deer or maybe a group of deer spent a good bit of time in the spot, but may not habitually visit there or it could be that deer traverse it several times daily. Tracks that come from different directions leading to the area, tracks over tracks from the opposite direction, and tracks in varying stages of decay evincing varied age all are indicative of a frequently used spot. Nocturnally deposited imprints can lure hunters to locales where no deer have been in daylight hours in months so, for our lands, it is wise to be skeptical of voluminous spoor in open places after general gun season has begun. Beds of cattle and hogs can at times resemble deer beds, but usually one or two pinches of the surface of the bed site will produce a hair that identifies the species. Except in the latest part of the season in our swampwoods, droppings last so short of a time that they are of minor help in deciphering deer patterns. Nonetheless, any accumulations of them warrant careful consideration as routine bedding areas or sites where deer fed in a prolonged fashion. Browsing evidence can also indicate feeding areas, but can be obfuscated by the extensive browsing and grazing by cattle.

Most of our terrain, while it will show tracks here and there, rarely displays a prolonged trail of a deer and so the tendency of bucks to place their hind feet slightly more toward midline than their front hooves is not always easily noted. In sandy and muddy areas the characteristic dragging of the hooves of bucks shows up well, however the simplest determinate of the sex of the animal that created the track is size. Obviously, this is not always true. It is unlikely a track from a ninety pound buck would be noticeably different than that from a ninety pound doe. Our deer are smaller than those of most of America and our does average ninety to ninety-five pounds. A one hundred and twenty pound doe is considered quite large and the largest I've ever taken was one hundred and thirty. Meanwhile, the bucks we take average in the one fifties. Granted, we kill primarily larger bucks, but the point is that the bucks average sixty pounds more than the mature does or, in other words, the average weight of a mature buck is 66% greater than a mature doe. No doubt, an animal that much heavier will leave larger tracks. When a typically sized track is encountered, it could be evidence of a doe or young buck, but when a large track is found, I'm confidant a large buck passed that way. We now restrict our harvest to bucks that exceed certain antler requirements and it is unlikely a buck whose track is sized similar to a doe would meet these minimums. By the way, the weights I've quoted are for deer on the lands I've hunted the past fifteen years. Land just to the north, which gave me sport for many years in the past, yielded does and bucks of lesser heft and friends who hunt five miles east of me also report lighter deer. Trips to north Florida have resulted in heavier whitetails. The point is that the average weights mentioned were for one small region, not for Florida as a whole.

On the subject of size, a word about our antlers is in order. The racks that seem outstanding here would, no doubt, not impress hunters from many other regions. A rack scoring one hundred inches is unusual enough to warrant recognition in the Florida Big Buck Registry. The point being is that everything is relative and Floridians get the same sense of accomplishment and achievement out of taking a buck that is better than average here as hunters do anywhere and how the rack compares to whitetails of far away is a concept not terribly unlike how it compares to mule deer or elk racks. The age of bucks can perhaps better equate deer from all regions for few bucks live five or more years without gaining habits and insights that make hunting them exceedingly difficult.

Scrapes and rubs are easily recognizable evidence of bucks. Most scrapes are visited at night, but I have seen them both initialized and freshened many times in broad daylight. A large number of the scrapes here are in sandy soil and often under oak branches. Rarely, will I hunt over a scrape as the only sign of buck presence, but the ones in the sand are worth sitting over after an early morning rain as bucks seem inclined to reopen them after such showers. Oddly, this tendency is not apparent in the scrapes in the black swamp earth or the dark soils along its edge.

Rubs can be found singly, in clusters, or in a fairly linear pattern. Again speaking only of the lands I hunt, the linear pattern of rubs or a pattern that parallels the curving fringes of swamps or heads usually evidences a trail a buck or bucks travel regularly and can be used to plan an effective ambuscade. Clusters of rubs, especially heavy concentrations of clustered rubs, are a manifestation of a buck's core area and often are near bedding sites. These, too, can be good to hunt at times, but require great caution because bucks seem quite cannily perceptive of incursions into these haunts. Recent evidence of continued habitation should be sought because a great number of the rubs are made before archery season begins. During the next six to eight weeks, the bucks are chasing does and not necessarily frequenting these well rubbed hideaways. As the rut winds down, the bucks return to their secret and hidden realms, but, in the meantime, food sources and weather patterns have changed and core areas may have undergone a shift. During the extended rutting period, doe rich areas are probably the best choice for ambushing a good buck and it is worth the scouting effort to have several such places in mind. It goes against the grain to abandon rubs and scrapes and hunt where there is little buck sign, but if does favor the spot, one is apt to be rewarded in our archery season.

Many years ago, I read an article that quoted Fred Bear declaring that he preferred stands with as distant a view as possible so that if he wasn't in a spot teaming with opportunity, he might at least see places with greater deer activity where he could try that afternoon or the next day. During rifle season, when the hunter density increases and deer sightings dwindle until, if not for the tracks, one might conclude there were no deer around, tighter and more secluded stand sites are more productive as pressured bucks ghost through the thickest coverts and only uncommonly expose themselves to the risks of more open terrain. While bow season is in progress, however, I follow Fred's advice for his reason and a couple others. The wide, encompassing view also allows me to see game that may be called or stalked. Many times, I've descried deer, hogs, or turkeys from an elevated stand and after studying the probable course, the landscape, and some easily distinguishable features, executed exciting and, at times, productive stalks. Other times, I've been able to lure remote animals within range by issuing bleats or grunts with my mouth or clicking, clacking, or grinding antlers together. As mentioned elsewhere in the text, if a buck is scent trailing a doe, in my experience, there is little chance of dissuading him with any calls so I trundle down and launch an interceptive stalk. Because of the desirability of slipping quietly and quickly from a stand, at this time of the year, fixed stands (chain or strap on or ladder stands) function best. Climbing stands have the advantage of not having to contaminate the area before the hunt and by the ease and silence of set up and my Lone Wolf has won my favor not only for its ease and quietness, but for the integrity of the company that manufactures it. However, I wait to use it when the chance of having to abandon the stand and commence a stalk diminishes which is usually at the end of bow season. Sometimes during the archery season, my stand is more like an observation and command center from which game is espied and multiple hunts are planned and initiated without any animal venturing within arrow range of the stand itself.

As most hunters are aware, whitetails can be called and at times as readily as turkeys or elk or other animals that are more often considered conducive to calling. Does respond to bleats throughout the year, but with especial alacrity from April to November and, years ago, before I learned the wisdom of not calling, I was amazed by how many I could call in with my not terribly authentic mouth bleats. Multiple times, deer that spooked from my truck in open pastures trotted back to investigate a trembling bleat despite the truck being in full view. One June day when my daughter was eight months old, I carried her about a cypress dome dotted pasture and came upon a muddy, stagnant pond. Breanna loved water and strained to reach it, but concerns about the water's potability and 'gators caused me to restrain her and she began to cry. We were completely without cover, but, nonetheless, three does raced up solicitously and eyed us from twenty-five yards. Perhaps her cries resembled a fawn's bleat, but I wonder if just the sound of a distressed young creature evokes either their curiosity or their maternal instinct and maybe that is why my bleats, far from realistic, work well. As further support of this notion, several times does have run right up to my hidden form when I'm screaming for coyotes.

Grunts call does, too, but only infrequently. The majority of the ones that have come to my grunts did so with such obvious eagerness that I suspect they had been separated from a companion and were seeking reunion. Most often, does have ignored my grunts even when they are in the immediate vicinity of my stand and the grunt is proffered to a distant buck. Rather than carry more gear and gadgets, I grunt with my throat and mouth and, as anyone who tries it will discover, it is not difficult to produce several different tones and types of grunts. By the way, does also utilize grunts for communication and hearing a deer grunt is by no means an assurance that the deer is a buck.

Most often I grunt as an attempt to entice an out of range buck closer. Success occurs fairly often as long as one bears the wind in mind. Typically, bucks will skirt downwind. The more directly upwind the buck is when one grunts, the greater the likelihood he will pass within close range of one's stand. Once again, this is not as critical for rifle hunters. I have also found that bucks that have passed one's stand and continued on have a tendency to return to a grunt without necessarily circling to a downwind position. Several times bucks have slipped by me before I was ready for a shot either because of the thickness of the cover or the rapidness of their gait (or maybe my unpreparedness?) and nearly always they retraced their steps after my grunt.

Rattling has also been very effective in luring bucks close enough for a bow shot for me. Like with using grunts, most of my rattles are to bucks that are in view and are situated where it is not likely they can or will get downwind of my stand. Circling to a downwind position is instinctive to a deer and this inclination is a major obstacle to success for a rattling bowhunter and needs to be born in mind before meshing the antlers. Rattling carries a further distance than grunts and for me has been more often helpful in tricking big bucks.

Most people know that the antibiotics that became available in the last eighty years seemed wonderful and it appeared they would wipe out diseases that had plagued mankind. Now doctors have learned the overuse of them has fostered resistance in bacteria that have been repeatedly exposed to them and medical personnel wish the antibiotics had been reserved for only the cases when they were truly required. A parallel can be drawn with deer calling whether it is with bleats, grunts, or rattled antlers. As enlightening and entertaining as it is to call and practice on young bucks or as tempting as it is to try to rattle a grand buck in from a position where it is nearly certain he will get one's wind, it should be recognized that each episode educates the deer. Then, when a hunter has a real chance at the grand old buck or when the young deer has matured into a dandy buck, that education may make him impossible to call. At that point, a hunter, like a doctor with an ineffective antibiotic, will wish he had not squandered calls inconsequentially. This concern to avoid introducing the connection between deer sounds and human presence to deer, renders me reluctant to rattle or grunt blindly although there is a fair potential to lure a buck standward. The probability that the unseen buck will either be in a downwind position or will circle downwind is high and the chance of an unseen buck blundering in within handy bow range unaware is minuscule. I sometimes overcome my restraint when features of the terrain coalesce to decrease the opportunity for a buck to sidle downwind and I've been rewarded on occasion as demonstrated elsewhere in this volume. Still, I think of grunts and rattles as most helpful as tools to coax sighted bucks closer.

A methodology that has been an invaluable component of my scouting is the creation of maps. Having traced the important features and borders of a hunting area from an aerial photograph or topographic map, I shrink the image to standard paper size and then make lots of copies, thirty or more. When a friend, unfamiliar with the land, accompanies me, I can give him or her a copy and even sketch ideas or routes on it. However, the primary purpose of the maps is to record information and one map will display piney woods, ponds, oak stands, scrubs, palmetto flats, creek strands, and all the assorted terrains. Using a set of marking pens or pencils of assorted hues, everything is color coded. Another will feature mast sources again utilizing various colors to depict locations of orange trees, cabbage palms, gallberries, persimmons, and oaks. The oaks are differentiated as well so in the years when the live oaks that produce the long, nearly black acorns that deer seem to cherish are dropping, a quick glance at the map will remind me of several definite spots worth scouting. Or when live oaks with the green acorns or the scrub oaks with round, brown acorns are sought after, another look will recommend several places and some of them may not have been in my thoughts for years. When scouting or roaming hunting lands and a type of favored deer food is encountered, I think I'll remember it the next time it is a preferred forage, but experience has demonstrated that while some such places stay in mind, others are lost. Maps capture and hold them readily accessible. Besides habitats and food sources, I have maps for buck sign and buck sightings, funnel locations, and still hunting routes. Most of the maps are updated yearly.

Gear is going to vary from region to region and from individual to individual. Here are the items I find worth carrying. Binoculars rate high and without them I feel handicapped. The more light gathering capability they have, the better, not because of a desire to hunt after legal hours, but because they are useful in many ways. For instance, I rely on recognition of distinctive trees or other terrain features rather than using trails blazed with ribbons or reflective tacks or employing electronic gismos, so in the predawn blackness the light gathering binoculars aid tremendously in finding the way to my stand site. Not having an established trail enables a hunter to take various routes to an area depending upon wind direction. A compass is always in my pocket and is useful in pinpointing a place or downed game and also for recording information that might help when blood trailing. My pockets also contain a knife, a diaphragm turkey call, a predator call, and a spare broadhead. One arrow in my quiver is headed with a judo point or hex head blunt and should my quiver become too much diminished, I can exchange heads thus augmenting the number broadheaded arrows. These days I carry a small flashlight in my pocket as well. Prior chapters may seem at odds with this, but that is because for many years I did not tote a flashlight or assigned the light to a pack that was only carried on occasion. My bows have light feathers tied to each end to manifest air movement. As mentioned earlier, my arrows and broadheads are heavy. Overall, I endeavor to bring as little as possible and still feel adequately supplied.

Some hunters grunt or whistle or make other noises to stop moving deer, facilitating the aiming process and I have used the technique years ago, but have abandoned it except in rare circumstances. Perhaps the instinctive style of my archery does not demand as stationary a target, or my arrows travel too slowly or I miss often enough to heartily appreciate a second chance. My experiences have demonstrated an increased frequency of deer jumping the string when thus alerted and noise halted deer almost never allow additional shots when missed. These deer, of course are at close range and the situation is probably much different for rifle hunters with more distant animals. An unalarmed, walking deer may duck or flinch with the sound of the bow, but most often then stands still and surveys the area for the cause of the noise. The number of times deer, even mature bucks, have allowed me multiple shots is noteworthy even if it does not reflect well on my skills with a bow and arrow. My journal contains several such occurrences and an excerpt will afford an example (the next chapter offers another noteworthy instance):

"Yesterday afternoon was windy and clear and fairly cold. I saw a wood duck from my stand and that was about all until a quarter to six (darkness now falls about 6:25). Two squirrels climbed gingerly and even quietly down a tree. Then nothing more moved. At 6:04 I decided to call it a day. Daylight still remained, but I had used chest waders to cross the creek and nearly submerged them and now wanted to recross with enough light to avoid going under. While disengaging the speedlight flash from the camera, my ears caught the familiar splush, splash, splush and I looked up to see two does ambulating toward me. I slipped the camera into my pack and readied Deer Bane.

"The biggest doe turned broadside at twelve yards. I bent the Widow with focus and concentration. Everything felt right and I told myself to release, but just then she took a step closer so now she was quartering toward me. There was no hurry and I should have waited and picked a spot and focused again, but instead I hastily tried to readjust and let go. The arrow slid under her and she jumped and stopped and angled her head back to peer behind her. She was still no more than fifteen yards off, but some limbs complicated the shooting opportunity and by now the other doe which was also fairly large was only nine yards to the west of my stand. I launched an arrow under her as well. She sprang a yard or two off and scanned the area, her body broadside to my tree. The large doe came closer again and, like her companion, was looking around, but she was nearly head on so, with a third arrow on the string, I drew Deer Bane and, taking my time, concentrated on part of the chest of the smaller doe. This arrow seemed to take flight of its own accord and zipped through her chest. She bounded off twenty-five yards, stopped, and looked about. The big doe ran five yards toward her and likewise halted and studied the area. The stricken doe exploded into action and hurled herself back toward me and fell lifelessly within a few yards of where she was shot.

"I had work in front of me with the high water and mud so I climbed down immediately and had success avoiding the deeper portions of the creek. The doe weighed 96 pounds."

Because much of the swampwoods is beyond the range of vehicles, toting downed deer is of interest. There are several ways to make a pack of the carcass. The technique I learned as a youngster and have employed for many years is to use a knife to cut the skin circumferentially around each foot between the hooves and the dew claws and then skin the leg up to the first major joint (half way up the leg). The joint is severed and the leg bone with the attached hooves removed. The dew claws remain on the skin which, in turn, remains continuous with the upper portion of each leg. The skin of the right hind leg is tied to that of the left foreleg with a simple overhand knot and likewise with the left rear and right fore. The dew claws prevent the knots from slipping. I prefer to carry the head on my left side so I slip the skin from the left hind leg over my right shoulder and that from the left foreleg over my left. This makes a reasonably comfortable pack with wide, soft straps and my left hand supports the head to keep it from bouncing against my leg. A deer can be carried miles this way (although to my shoulders the straps seem to lose their softness after a half mile or so which is funny because upon examining the skin, no changes are evident and it still appears soft and supple!) Another advantage of this method is that since the belly points upwards, it can be used on a dressed deer without being uncomfortable or exceptionally messy. If one does desire to gut the deer, it is easiest to do so before deboning the lower legs as this enables the hunter to stand on the spread legs during the dressing process. By the way, with all these toting methods, placing blaze orange on the animal when carrying it should be considered.

I enjoy reading about hunting of all kinds and one book of African adventures described the manner natives there utilized to transport game. The skin of each foreleg is slit from the same joint mentioned above halfway down to the hoof and then the joint is severed with care not to cut the skin. The skin is pulled from the upper half of the now unattached leg bone resulting in the skin joining that of the upper leg and connecting it loosely to the disjointed bone at mid-length with the skin still on the bone from the midpoint down to the hoof and the bone bare above that to the severed joint. Slits are cut between the upper leg bone and the hamstrings of the hind legs and the loose foreleg bone is inserted through this slit, left to left and right to right. When the skin attached to the front legs is pulled taunt, the bone tightens 'T' fashion against the rear leg and thereby cannot fit back through the slit. The hunter's arms slide behind the skin of the foreleg and under the front of the hind leg so the deer drapes head down on the hunter's back and the meaty rear legs rest on his shoulders. I have used this carry often, but only for shorter distances. Its main advantage is the speed of preparation, taking but a minute or two while the earlier mentioned method requires several minutes to prepare. Disadvantages include the fact that getting into the pack is troublesome and the head swinging between the toter's legs can cause tripping yet the head is at an awkward position to hold. Also, field dressing renders the burden lighter, but less comfortable.

Later, I read Larry Koller's book <u>Shots at Whitetails</u> and learned of another variation. Slits are cut into all four legs like one would for hanging a deer on a gambrel. The front legs are entered into the slits of the rear legs on the same side and then small branches, maybe eight inches in length, are slipped into the cuts in the front legs to ensure they can't slide out of position. In this case, the front legs rest on the bearer's shoulders. The stems of cabbage palms serve well as the short sticks and are readily cut with only a knife. Like with the African method, the preparation is rapid and simple. I find it easier to load a deer thus prepped on my back than the African way and with the head up, the tote itself is less clumsy and trammeling. Again, if the distance is long, the pack method first described is worth the extra time required to effectuate it.

If any topic can get opinions flying about at a hunt camp, it is the moon's influence on deer activity with hunters weighing in on all sides of the issue. So often hunters hear about the moon providing enough light for deer to feed all night. Two facts should be considered. First, deer eyes are so adept at gathering light that starlight is easily adequate to allow them to feed and they even feed on cloudy nights. Second, it is not characteristic for deer to feed the entire night, but rather for periods alternating with intervals of bedding.

I recorded the times of all deer sightings for many years and, with thousands of bits of data, compared daylight deer activity to moon phases. The greatest activity was associated with no moon, but full moon days ranked in the second position and were only barely inferior. Three-quarter moon produced the least sightings. This data also allowed me to analyze the accuracy of feeding time tables. (By the way, John Alden Knight, who originated the first such table, dubbed Solunar, began his contemplation of periods of heightened feeding while fishing near the source of the St. Johns River here in Florida, not far from my hunting lands.) Although the tables did demonstrate a slightly greater number of sightings than would be expected from equal segments of random time, it was enlightening to see how often deer were moving in times other than those predicted. The tables were most accurate when their predicted times fell within the two hours after first or before last light.

More of my thoughts and ideas on hunting are found scattered throughout the pages of this book, particularly in the chapters on airy hunts and blood trailing. I have opinions and habits touching upon all aspects of hunting including times and days to hunt, hats and clothing, camouflage patterns, quivers, fletching and nock colors and more, but they really are just personal preferences or locally applicable. The thing I can stress as being important to all hunters is knowledge of the game animal and its habits. Keen observation of whitetails in the wild offers the foremost instruction and I attribute the greatest share of my learning to a decision twenty some years ago to limit my hunting weapons to traditional bows. For many years I would not launch an arrow more than twenty yards, and sometimes no more than fifteen and only then at stationary and unobstructed targets that distant. Therefore, most of the time for all those years, I did nothing more than closely observe a great number of deer. Later, I began photographing out of range deer and, later still, videoing them. These video recordings were even more helpful because they could be studied minutely, repeatedly, and at great length. So much can be thus exposed about deer behavior including alertness and occurrences that arouse attention, feeding tendencies, patterns and routes, submissive and dominant postures and conducts, deer-deer interactions, deer-other animal interactions, postural indications of the animal's next action, feeding activity, and so much more. Even someone who desired only to be a better and more consistent gun hunter would do well to restrict themselves to a primitive bow or embrace a vow to take no longer than a fifteen yard shot for two seasons no matter what temptations presented. The change in the spots hunted coupled with the intimate observations would forever influence one's approach to hunting.

15

The Lucky Buck

Having come so far, dear reader, there is no doubt that you appreciate that while I take archery seriously and, because of my dedication and love of the sport, I endeavor to practice and improve my skills, nonetheless my shooting proficiency could hardly be classified expert and good is probably a stretch. You have read of complete misses at short ranges and empty quivers after successive unsuccessful chances not much greater than ten yards distant. I must own up to misses not yet divulged to you that have occurred when animals were nearly touching my stand's tree, two and a half yards away, four yards away and most likely any distance out to twenty-five yards. It is not easy to imagine anyone missing more than I have. With that in my mind, I hope you won't begrudge me reminiscing over a few of my most noteworthy and spectacular shots before the main part of the story which is certainly less than flattering to my archery ability. By the way, the story compliments my friend Mack's bowmanship no more than mine, but I can offer testimony that he is one of the most natural and most accurate instinctive archers I have met.

One night, as dusk progressed and the range of vision dwindled, a grey boar trotted across a pasture toward some tubs of molasses placed out for the cattle. As he neared the first tub, he spun and lit out in the classic hog manner with his short legs stretching ahead in rapid, little, graceless bounds either spooked by my stalk or by scent we left as we approached the tubs. Choosing a looping course, he scudded away at a rapid pace and, without thought, I drew Deer Bane and let the hard string spring from my fingers. There was not enough twilight left to follow the going shaft despite the bright fletchings and even the shape of the speeding hog at forty-five or fifty yards was vague and indistinct. The sound was right however; a heavy ssshunk and even though he seemed too distant for us to hear his thudding retreat, a moment or two after the thick, muffled sound of the striking arrow, the pasture rested too quietly in a sudden and unnatural silence. Just after the release, the boar, in my eyes, had dissipated from view, a hazy and dissolving apparition. My friend's eyes were younger and sharper, so when he told me the boar took a faster, tighter, more desperate fish hook of a run after the arrow with its curving trajectory reached him, we strode northward to investigate. The boar was dead. The arrow that had seemingly leapt from the bow so far forward of his running form and vanished into the gloom midway into its arcing flight had transfixed him perfectly, driving through his ribs and both lungs and spilling into the empty night beyond.

The evening was not yet concluded for as we walked back from my kill, the moonlight illuminated the black forms of two hogs making for the tubs. They were both good sized and my companion scurried closer, low to the ground, to intercept them. I followed five or eight yards behind with an arrow nocked for should his shot only wound a hog a second quarrel might shorten and facilitate the blood trail. When the hogs passed broadside at fifteen to twenty yards, my friend released and once again the sound was right. The black shapes scrabbled away at top speed at first side by side and then one inched ahead. I drew drawing bead in my mind's eye on the leading silhouette, but then, doubt assailing me, let off and asked, "Your hog is the lead one, right?"

"No, the rear one."

They were now fifty yards out, but with the solid blackness of their forms and the heightened moonlight of the advancing night, they were readily visible. Deer Bane's limbs bent and the unfathomable ability of the brain to calculate the speeds and courses of two objects took over and though it was still too dark to see the arrow's flight, the result was obvious for, concurrently with the thud of the impacting arrow, the hindmost hog tumbled, flipped and then became a silent, still black hump in a pasture of vague hues and soft shadows. Palmettos a handful of yards beyond swallowed the lead hog nearly immediately.

My arrow had struck the juncture of the neck and chest of the fleeing hog and broke a vertebrae. Our good cheer on the heels of the fortuitous shot was tempered somewhat by the discovery of a blood trail extending beyond the fallen pig and into the palmettos evidencing that the injured hog was the foremost one after all so despite the miraculous flight and result of my arrow, our next couple hours were spent puzzling out a scant and difficult trail.

Only two arrows flew from Deer Bane that night and both seemed remarkable to me. Many of my memorable shots have occurred sequentially as if all things were in harmony and shooting was totally natural. Accuracy is so simple and easy at these times that I'm convinced it will be that way continuously from that point on and later, when faced with inaccuracy or inconsistency, bewilderment takes hold. One day arrows find their mark almost as if willed or guided there and the next no amount of concentration or effort proves fruitful.

I had another 'on' spell one night at our camp several years ago. Don Davis and I had wandered to Craig's pavilion and pretended we were going to launch arrows at a small orange stuck into our backstop at a good long distance, at least forty-five yards and possibly nearing sixty. With traditional equipment, it wasn't within our normal range at all, but somehow upon drawing Deer Bane deeply, I was imbued with a sense of confidence and let the feathered shaft whisk off through the night. The orange could not have been centered more perfectly. Our camp is composed almost entirely of rifle hunters, but this shot got a few guys enthused enough to shoot some arrows at the target. We chose more normal ranges like ten to fifteen yards, but the confidence and unconscious precision remained with me and I consistently hit nickels at these distances.

When a tremendous buck steps out and the opportunity is at hand, but will disappear any second, the nervousness and urgency can erode a bowhunter's confidence and distract him from the routine of his normal shooting habits. The opposite can happen as well. A lack of strong desire to take an animal can let the bowman settle into a shot with no nerves and all his concentration on the process rather than the outcome. As an example, one still hunting afternoon, I spotted a few black hogs fifty to seventy yards away. My gear had already been packed and my truck was loaded to head home and now I wondered if I really wanted a hog since it would require returning to the camp to clean it and hang it in the cooler which, coupled with the time spent driving there, would hold me back an hour at least and more likely an hour and a half. Also, no boars were visible in the group and typically I held out for boars. On the other hand, I had tromped and searched through a great portion of our hunting lands starting early this morning and now that hogs were finally in view, did I truly want to walk away from them?

The debate played back and forth through my head and the solution I adopted doesn't make sense even now in retrospect, but somehow the notion of turning the decision over to fate had an appeal at the time and I convinced myself to attempt no stalk, but if, with but a single arrow from the fullest present distance, the largest sow could be stricken, then so be it. There was no nervousness nor anxiety as I drew Daddy; no concern for the outcome, in fact it was like a detached indifference, more like a vaguely interested spectator than an involved participant. As you have no doubt surmised, the arrow arced unerringly to the beast and drove completely through her so perfectly that despite her immediate efforts to evacuate the pasture at utmost speed, she made it less than twenty yards.

The shot was effortless and the results ideal, but what if my heart had been set on securing the sow? I'll never know, but the lack of a pounding heart and the ease of each of the constituent portions of the act of drawing, pointing, and releasing the shaft makes me wish that, the next time a monstrous buck approaches, I could convince myself that I don't really care whether he ends up in the back of my truck or not!

In the preceding accounts I've chronicled three hogs taken at ranges I consider long and yet the penetration of the arrow was marked. One broadhead was stopped by solid and destructive contact with the spine, but the other two arrows passed completely through the thick animals (hogs being typically thicker than deer, especially boars with their heavy, cartilaginous shield.) I've stated earlier my belief in heavy arrows and these examples demonstrate how much energy the weighty shafts carry with them. Light arrows lose more and more ability to penetrate as distance increases, but the heavy missiles lose proportionally much less. The increased speed of lighter shafts is initially appealing as it offers flatter trajectories, but the costs can be reduced penetration and, despite the faster flight, a greater incidence of deer jumping the string because the light arrows do not dampen the sharpness of the bow's noise as well.

Another remarkable arrow flight should be mentioned here. Several years ago, having casually promised someone a hog to barbecue, anxious to try a new bow, (ordered eighteen months before with a promised delivery of six weeks, but only arriving two days before this hunt), and with expectations of nothing but a short and routine effort, I was stymied by a mystifying lack of hogs and sign as if a mass departing migration had taken place. Finally, after hours of searching, I caught sight of three sows. There was no cover so the stalk was tricky and conducted more on my belly than my feet, but at last I was within fifteen yards. A couple of piglets bustled among the feeding sows and, desiring to make no orphans, I delayed drawing my little bow Bent Medicine until I became certain to which hog or hogs they belonged. The larger of the two black sows was the mother, but no sooner had this become apparent than the hogs strode directly away from me toward a wooded dike in single file. They traveled steadily for two hundred yards and despite the openness of the pasture, I did not fall too far behind for they never milled about or looked back. Upon reaching the shaded hump of the dike they spread about for a minute causing me to slow my renewed stalk and return to my hands and knees. By the time I was again close, the brown hog fed over the dike and out of sight. The two black ones walked apart for a moment and then up to one another and sunk to the ground rolling onto their sides twelve yards from where I knelt. The larger one, with her belly toward me and her piglets nursing, was closest, but the other was so near her that no avenue to the furthest hog's vitals was not protected by the body of the nearer. I bided the time hoping for a shift of their positions, but receiving instead, after ten minutes or more, a shift of the wind and they were up and hoofing toward the dike in the blink of an eye! I have already confessed in the chapter on bows that I never developed a feeling for consistent precision with Bent Medicine so I doubt that a lack of familiarity will suffice as a good excuse for my arrow jetting at least two feet over the back of the scrambling hog only fifteen or sixteen yards away. The arrow disappeared over the dike and the racing hogs followed suit. I bounded up the sandy sides as well hopeful of maybe one more opportunity, but the sight I beheld confounded me. Fifty or more yards beyond the dike, the brown hog was spinning around, squarely skewered by my errant shaft. She bolted into the woods startled by my sudden appearance or by the galloping thuds of her companions. She collapsed in less than forty yards. While the other sows bedded, she must of have fed out into exactly the wrong place and then my arrow, wildly missing its mark and arching over the dike, descended perfectly into her chest.

That was the first game taken with Bent Medicine and it is the only bow I know that killed two animals unwittingly. The second time was in Colorado when, making my way through an area of low, scraggly vegetation and desirous of some practice, I picked a small and distinctive branch of pale sage as a target. The arrow's flight was susurrous and precise and with satisfaction I hastened to retrieve it only to find a writhing, but fatally wounded snake tangled about the sage and the shaft.

During some mid-day scouting, Mack and I passed a marshy pond and I noted a bull frog, fairly large for our territory, on the far bank, partially out of the water and facing away from us. Frogs have good eyesight, skittish natures, and once startled do not offer second chances so a stalk would have been a risky undertaking. His distance was twenty yards. With a less than perfect shot he would achieve the shelter of the mud and water and even if mortally injured would be impossible to find. A broadhead or judo point would increase the wound size and thereby diminish the chance of keeping him from escape, so I selected an arrow tipped with a field point. Bane Too drew smoothly and before I realized I had released, the arrow was hissing toward the target and impaled him so perfectly that he never jerked or flinched, his spine severed directly aft of his head. From nose to toes he measured thirteen and a half inches.

With my Lone Wolf stand, I climbed a tree in the Tyson Creek swamp. At the base of the tree, rolled up to minimize escaping scent, were the chest waders that enabled me to wade the deeper portions of the creeks and leave as little olfactory evidence of my passing as possible. Two flocks of turkeys converged sixty or more yards to the southwest and excited 'pucks' and 'clucks' and cackles went on for more than a half hour. During this interval three hogs trotted through the area. Time passed and I updated my journal until movement fifty yards off captured my attention. Binoculars revealed antlers through the ferns. The buck's feeding pattern, although haphazard, eventually eased him away from my stand so I proffered two soft grunts which had no noticeable effect upon him, but a doe ambulated briskly to within two yards of my tree's base. Her deliberate approach may have been only coincidental for she gave no indication of searching for another deer and began feeding on water oak acorns with no hesitation, remaining quite close for ten or more minutes. Gradually, the territory she sniffed for acorns shifted to the south.

I still held a doe tag, but was reluctant to attempt a shot for, even though the probability was looking scantier all the time, I also held hope the buck might yet meander toward the stand. In the meantime, he had grown quite distant and finally several minutes elapsed without the tiniest glimpse of him or even movement in the ferns. The doe was now more than forty yards away although her circling pattern of feeding brought her slightly closer at intervals. Directing the arrow point toward her, I drew Bane Too from time to time as little openings in the limbs and brush allowed, but only as practice and with no intentions of consummating the shot because of the great distance and because of all the obstacles restricting avenues for arrow flight. Once when she was facing directly away, two raccoons ambled past and she remained motionless, staring at them. I pretended a shot again and then let up, but deep inside I felt I could have made that shot. Tree trunks and limbs formed a small triangular window where, if the arrow traveled perfectly true, the broadhead would surely drive into her mediastinum and, if the flight was errant, the limbs would intercept it and shield the doe from a wounding hit. Fortified by these thoughts, I drew Bane Too again, this time with different and deadly intentions, providing I could achieve the same level of self-assurance and certainty. I relished the power my muscles sensed in the bow's bent limbs. Perhaps as a result of the preceding dry runs, my only thoughts were those of surety and confidence and the release was quick, smooth, and quiet. The feathered shaft slipped easily through the diminutive wood bordered triangle and even the fletchings disappeared into the brownish fur of the doe. Exploding into action, she ran a small loop and fell in the creek quite near the base of my tree, perishing scant seconds after the arrow struck.

The broadhead scarcely protruded from the front of her chest leaving me doubtful of a good blood trail if it had come to that. Happily, it was unnecessary. The arrow had buried into her lengthwise, entering just above the hip bone on her right side and exiting the chest barely left of midline slicing both lungs, the aorta, and the pulmonary arteries en route. The shaft was undamaged and she was the third whitetail in a row that particular arrow had claimed and the fourth consecutive deer for the broadhead.

Theodore Roosevelt wrote about rifle marksmanship that many, many poor shots have been fired for each of the notable ones, but the successes are those that stick in our memories while the failures sift through like minnows too slender for the weave of a net, leaving us with a skewed impression of our abilities. His opinion holds true for bowshots as well and arrow flights like the ones I've sketched above are those upon which I prefer to dwell, but unfortunately too many other shots remind me of my limitations and buffer any tendency toward overconfidence. It is time to get to the meat of the chapter.

Mack and I had each emptied quivers at bucks earlier one archery season. After four misses, Mack's fifth and last arrow slayed a resplendent whitetail. A couple days later, a fine nine point followed and worried three does in a palmetto and scrub dotted pasture within sight of my stand and, slipping down, I initiated a stalk, ending up on my knees behind a palmetto with the does no further than fifteen yards and the buck about twenty-five. Fearful of imminent discovery, I pulled back Deer Bane's supple limbs and sent an arrow sailing well over his back. The 'thwap' of the bow elicited raised heads and intense alertness from all the deer. My next arrow glanced off one of the buck's bourbon colored tines and rattled against another as it careened up and away. This caused the does to run on beyond me and the buck to bound back a few paces. He then stepped cautiously toward me bent on rejoining the other deer. One doe also came back from the opposite direction and was on the far side of a short palmetto clump maybe six or eight yards from me. Half drawn and waiting for the buck to offer more of a broadside presentation, yet at the same time the target of the doe's suspicious and knowing stares, I felt the time was now or never and, completing the draw, sent another feathered missile somewhere into the pasture in the general vicinity of the buck. The doe was off at once, but the buck, with a hesitant and nervous gait, angled toward the other does and did not distance himself from me in the least. He was completely broadside now, but my final broadheaded arrow cut nothing but air. The buck stopped now and looked intently at my sheltering fronds. I hastened to detach a judo point and affix my spare broadhead, but he decided to linger no longer and raced to the does and then the little group skittered across the pasture and out of sight.

Mack and I traded our similar stories on our way to a whitetail haunt in Bull Creek and I envied his tale's ending. He climbed a stand in the murk of the pre-dawn creek woods and I waded across the swamp and set up a few hundred yards away. A deer blew from Mack's general direction at seven-thirty, but there was no deer action and truthfully little action of any kind until nearly nine o'clock when a limping eight point made his way toward the skimpy islet just north of my tree. He favored one foreleg quite noticeably and, wondering if Mack had wounded him even though he arrived from the west and Mack was south, I scanned with binoculars, but failed to see a wound or scar. He fed diligently on acorns, a seemingly unlikely behavior in a freshly injured deer. His antlers were symmetrical and the pretty color of aged osage, but not extraordinarily heavy or wide. The slender points were long and graceful.

My first arrow's flight looked good, but slipped over the buck's back by the tiniest fraction. It smacked solidly and loudly into a fin-like projection of a cypress trunk and the startled buck jumped closer to me and scanned back toward the tree. I missent a second arrow in the same manner, ideally aimed right and left, but ever so slightly over the back. The buck no longer seemed at ease and as he strode off, Deer Bane and I whisked an arrow that was finally the correct height, but sadly flew behind him. This proved too much and he bolted.

That turned out to be the sum total of the morning's activity and at the designated time, I met Mack at his stand. He guided me verbally to some particular spots to look for arrows and I knew then that stories were forthcoming. The buck had come by him early and already limping. The three arrows Mack directed toward him had touched not a hair and, only mildly alarmed, the buck had blown and continued away to the northwest. "What a coincidence," I thought as I confessed my parallel unsuccessful efforts. "First we empty quivers on bucks we stalked and now, on the same morning, we each miss the same buck three times!"

As we discussed the buck on our trek to the truck, our early references called him 'The Limping Buck', but by the time we were slipping our bows and gear into the vehicle, I noted his title had progressed to 'The Lucky Buck'. Six arrows from hidden ambush, none at excessive distances, had failed to touch him. He was lucky, maybe because the arrows missed or maybe because of the archers he chose to pass. Maybe his limp was only evidence of another close call averted. One must wonder what coursed through his brain on this morning of peculiar thunks and hisses. Years have passed and as far as I know, no one has taken the Lucky Buck.

It is my hope, dear reader, that these chapters will have given you some pleasure and diversion, and also captured and conveyed some of beauty and wondrousness of nature, of whitetails, of their pursuit, and of archery. May all your sylvan times be special and memorable.

978-0-595-41362-1
0-595-41362-5